26 Doses

of

Career Triage

JANICE COLEMAN

DEDICATION

To all who meet the marketplace every day with the
expectations of being their BEST selves and being appreciated
for their BRILLIANCE

Table of Contents

Acknowledgements

I want to thank God Almighty without Whom I cannot do anything. I want also to acknowledge my family who continue to be a motivation to me as I work and strive to become the next best me. My expressions of thanks and appreciation to friends who have cheered me on through 'A LOT'. Additionally, to those without whom this work would not be needed, my clients, the students and other professionals in the marketplace seeking the BEST them they can be.

A collegial special thanks to all of the colleagues in this career industry that I have had over the years who have been with me/for me in the midst of my own career metamorphosis. Also a word of acknowledgment to the late sage, Richard Bolles. His powerful book, What Color is My Parachute, is the ultimate manual of this industry called career management. I have read many of his volumes which he diligently updated every single year from 1970 and it, in his passing, still continues to be produced to this day.

My heartfelt thanks to Marlyn Kalitan for taking a pen to this work and tightened it up for the second printing. You are a gem!

Continued blessings to all!

26 Doses of Career Triage

Foreword

I have been in the "people" side of the business for my entire career. Leading people to reach their full potential has been an inherent goal in the many roles I played in both my corporate career and certainly in my last 20 years in consulting. We often lament that life is a journey…so is a career. I have long professed that it is incumbent on each individual to manage and grow their career. To achieve this, we need to take control, take risk and take advantage.

Just a few words about my journey…I navigated the corporate ladder successfully earning a reputation as an astute business "fixer" and "starter". I was often tapped on the shoulder to handle the next crisis and thrived on the challenge. About 20 years into my career I was tapped by someone outside the corporate world offering me the chance to lead an entrepreneurial organization. I took control, took the risk and I am still taking advantage of a great career.

Janice, although beginning her career as an IT professional, steered her career into assisting others to find the best version of their professional self. She did that deliberately. She found her passion and acquired the skills she needed to succeed in a career that offered others what she found through her career journey. In her book, 26 Doses of Career Triage, she offers her prescription for success based on her career trials, tribulations and training. Janice brings the reader on her journey and creates relatability for the reader to plot their own voyage.

Today's workforce is faced with a lot of unknowns. It also has 4 generations within the workforce. There is a call to action to upskill, remain current and be prepared for augmentation and automation. There is a demand for knowledge transfer and knowledge exchange as the more tenured generations leave the workforce. Is this a challenge or an opportunity? It depends on how you perceive change and the future. Janice's practical advice in formulating career choices and paths is important for those traversing their future.

There is some "Carpe Diem" wisdom in the book, advising us to take advantage of what is available...to make choices...to take risk...to stretch. Above all, she guides the reader to formulate a plan. To create an efficacious plan, you must know yourself to be the best version of yourself. Interspersed among words of wisdom and encouragement is strategic, empirical and tactical actions the reader can take in starting a career, enhancing a career, recreating a careering, and exiting a career.

The most valuable lesson is it's up to you...you own your journey and it is your ride. So, if you are looking to find the "cure-all" for the career blues, you should take a few doses of Janice's remedies.

Thanks for trusting me to write the foreword for your book.

Sharon Imperiale, CEO, CCI Consulting

Preface

I use the word 'excited' so much that I think that anyone reading this preface, or who knows me personally would think, "She's always excited." Well, I am! I am EXCITED to bring this message to you. I do not take for granted that you are reading these words I have been inspired to write. Also, I acknowledge the time you will spend in reading this book.

The pages of 26 Doses have been around long enough. It is now here.

Of course, I have been reading books for many years. In my practice of doing, one thing that I often did not do was to read the preface of books, and rarely would I read anything that comes before chapter 1 simply because I wanted to get right into it. But that will not be the case from now on. Why? Because in my preparation for this book, I have now learned the purposefulness of each section of the book. Mercy! What I have been missing all of my life! Yes, I was in the dark. But, now I see the light.

The preface is the setup for a book and it contains different types of information to help the reader of the book understand the book thoroughly. It is the author's opportunity to prep the audience for greater comprehension and more functional use of the material before them. As varied as each book is, so can the preface be. You, my audience, will be more ready to see through my eyes in this wonderful world of careers and how you can be more confident in it as you grow and develop into the person and professional you are designed to be.

That said, I will share with you some vital information now so that 26 Doses of Career Triage can do for you what it is truly capable of doing in changing the lives of its readers. There are going to be five sections in this preface that will guide/springboard you into the content of the book.

WHY ME?

Why is Janice a great person to share this message?

I will not start with where I was born and raised, you can see that in the biography. I will say, though, in hindsight, I could have been in any professional space and would have made it work. I think that many of us believe that. Yet, the premise for my 20 years in the career management field is that there is a place where each of us will thrive with the most ease. That's the place we all want to be.

I had been working since age 14 at various part-time jobs as many of us would say. I learned early that work was an important part of life. I did not know the importance of *well-suited* work until later on in life. Fast forward to my career in Information Technology (IT) where I had to have therapy, it was rewarding and well paying. I was there for over a decade. It was fun AND stressful. I did not want to keep up the pace of that ever-changing industry and I decided to move out of it. While I was in it, I became a member of Toastmasters International. I found that I loved to present and sought ways to make this a profession for myself. In 1999, I did what I, as a NOW career professional, would STRONGLY advise against. With the skills and guts I had, I jumped into the speaking profession. That was my transition. I had to make it work. This was not an easy course to have chosen. I was there. I stand today as a testament to the fact that things always work out for me, but I really could have done some things to make it easier for myself.

I started in the career management industry via a connection from a gentleman, Mark Plante who indeed is the consummate networker. He introduced me to his wife, Lauri, who worked for an international outplacement firm. She brought me on board as a career coach. She taught me the basis upon which I have built my ability to help professionals and students in their quest to find the job they truly love.

I have worked with individuals and groups; with private clients and as a 'coaching partner' with larger firms; on long-term projects and 'Hurry up, I need this job yesterday' projects. Over the past 20 years, I have been able to support so many people to become better employed by helping them become acquainted with who they really are and how to make their work match what they feel in their hearts about what having a career means to them.

I always encourage my clients and anyone that I share this Career Triage message with that they should not settle when they can go full steam ahead and establish a career that makes them happy and fits who they are becoming.

WHY YOU?

If you have made it this far in the preface, you will realize that I am just like you. I have had jobs that have turned me on and I have had jobs that have turned me off as well. I have been with companies that have helped me to grow and I have been in spaces that nearly choked the life out of me. I worked for managers who have been the quintessential leaders and I have LOVED them to life, AND I have worked for people who were so small and petty that I regret having said "Yes," to what was not the best for my well-being. I have lived through a lot. I am YOU.

I know that there may be a few reasons why you are reading this project right now:

- You are my family member/friend/colleague and you are showing your love and support.
- You are in a job that makes you crazy and you are ready to move out and on.
- You are new to the job market and you are going to get started right.
- You are out of work or underemployed and need some fuel to get moving.
- You are the consummate professional who is always learning.

All of these make sense to me. Regardless in which category you belong, there is something here for you. Whether you are looking for your first job, your next job or your last job, HOLD on and work through this book cover to cover and you will feel better about the whole thing called careers. Because there is hope and YOU can do something about it.

WHY THIS?

Why 26 Doses of Career Triage? It is a work of love for me. Almost every time I share the name of this my flagship program, I receive responses of intrigue. People get it. The byline Career Triage is, "If you feel like your career is in the ER and you are trying to keep from going to the morgue... You need triage."

There is nearly nothing else most commonly in ⚘ people's lives that can make them sicker than when they are in the wrong career OR at a job that is not a good fit. Some statistics say that more heart attacks happen on Sunday evenings and Monday mornings. Why? Um... The claim is stress related to work. We will not deliberate the point here, but I can get that. Stress because you have a job. Stress because you don't have a job. The dynamics around our career/employment can create many issues that can make us feel down on ourselves.

As I worked with professionals over the years, I noticed that I would go through the same process every time to get to the ultimate outcomes. One day, it dawned on me that my line of inquiry seemed very similar to that of the triage process we experience when we are going for emergency treatment. Webster's definitions of triage are:

> 1a : The sorting of and allocation of treatment to patients, especially battle and disaster victims according to a system of priorities is designed to maximize the number of survivors.
> b : The sorting of patients (as in an emergency room) according to the urgency of their need for care.
>
> 2 : The assigning of priority order to projects on the basis of where funds and other resources can be best used are most needed or are most likely to achieve success.

My comprehensive program is designed to determine where the client is and how to get them ready for a happy existence in the marketplace, whether that means a new job or more vitality with their current employer. I determine where we should go once agreed upon by the client we move ahead. The program components that cover a compliment of areas included in a GREAT professional toolkit are:

- Resume Recovery / Resume Rescue
- Self-Marketing Meds
- Interview Infusion
- Negotiating Needles
- Skills Pills
- Networking Nutrition

These in conjunction with the evaluation of social media

presence like LinkedIn and possibly ongoing coaching has served to put many professionals like you in the driver's seat regarding their career. These will not be covered in this work as standalone topics except Networking Nutrition.

This volume of 26 Doses of Career Triage is a small compilation of a HUGE work that coaches like me have at our disposable to give to their clients. Each and EVERY client is different and my responsibility is to identify the right complement and configuration of tools to support that specific client to reach their goals. It is IMPOSSIBLE to offer/share EVERYTHING with EVERYONE. It's not gonna happen. If it does… Um… that means that that client has been in TRIAGE way too long. So as not to seem morbid, I will just leave it at that. ☺

This is not a comprehensive work intended to be the be-all-end-all. It is a small useful tool to move you to be even more deliberate about your career. Admittedly, there are topics/subjects that overlap, and you will see that here. I will make references to a wide range of concepts to get my points across. Feel free to call me or GOOGLE anything that you are not familiar with and for which I may not have taken the time to expand upon for you here.

WHY NOW?

This is simple. Because it is time to make the necessary changes. I am sure that you have heard this a million times, "If not you. Who? If not this. What? If not now. When?" My friends, it's time out for suffering through because of the paycheck or any other thing that overrides the cry of our hearts to become that which we desire.

HOW TO GET THE MOST OUT OF THIS BOOK

Since you and I are not presently in a one-on-one, there is a concept in my head as to how you can use this book to help you as you continue to fortify your career on an ongoing basis. You will need a notebook dedicated to your efforts here!

Treatment Plan I

If you are new to the "world of work", use this book to help get started the 'right way' with the right perspective about the various aspects of your career. You should read through the entire book. Next, go back through the book and do the exercise(s) for each chapter. Use the lead quote for your affirmation/meditation time. Maintain a grow book for yourself that will help you to monitor your journey as you build your career 'muscles'. This process would take 26 weeks if you FOCUS on one chapter a week.

Treatment Plan II

If you are in a profession of five years or more and you are happy with your career and are seeking to fortify yourself, you should read through the entire book. Then go back and identify the one or two chapters that are areas of growth and let it resonate with you. Read through those chapters. One a week, complete exercise(s). Use the lead quote for your affirmation/meditation time. You can repeat this process to continue to refortify your career and employability factor.

Treatment Plan III

If you are a professional who is experiencing challenges with your current career/job, HURRY and read the book. ☺ Read doses x, x, and x. Do the exercises and use the lead quote for your affirmation/meditation time. You may want to contact me for a free consultation. **Let's begin!**

Our attitude toward life determines life's attitude toward us
– John N. Mitchell

Dose 1

Attitude

What self-respecting book about change and fortitude would not have a chapter about attitude? And since attitude is a GOOD 'A' word, here is what it's all about.

The word attitude in the nautical world is often used in relation to the direction of a vessel. They might say something like, "The attitude of the vessel is North by North East." This indicates the direction of the ship and where it is pointed. There is also this thing called "attitude control" which is the measures that are taken to keep the vessel on course. Skilled captains keep this in check to ensure the successful arrival at their destination.

First question of the day? What is your attitude? Where are you pointed? Guess what… Your words give you away. What is it that you say? And yes, how you say it will often be an indication of your attitude and where you are going in the purest sense.

We all can find ourselves in situations where the disposition of the room can influence our 'now' attitude. What do I mean? Well, have you ever gone to an event where the energy in the room was so HIGH? Everyone and everything in the room so hyped that they were literally in the stratosphere? The power is on and all attitudes are positive. Everyone is UP and there will be no stopping us "NOW". This is a wonderful thing. But this, by and large, is temporary because we all go home without the backdrop of the glitz and glamour or the music or the MOTIVATOR in the front of the room dropping pearls of wisdom that make us so excited.

A real experience like this would be one with Tony Robbins. That's right. Tony Robbins. You CANNOT get any more hype than him. Why? Not because he promotes this, but because he is what he is. He is an icon and has been for over 40 years. He has taken *change* to a whole new level. With this comes a certain attitude. I went to one of his events in New York City. My attitude changed simply from the thought of being in the same room with this man on stage. I saw him get people who would not want to be seen jumping up and down, yelling and swinging their hands in the air. WHY? Because of Tony's attitude. He said that a person who is more certain has the greater influence. The proof is in the pudding. I saw an entire convention floor of people on their feet at the peak of controlled insanity and I wasn't an exception. His attitude is one of FOCUS, ultra-positivity and "I can do it". This is an unbeatable combination. He emits such a feeling of power. Who wouldn't be influenced? If for no other reason the pressure of looking like rigamortis had set in, you're going to jump and yell being all present with the crowd of people around you. And this too can be temporary. When the endorphin levels return to normal and we go back home, we may be left with hundreds of dollars of resources which can be a good thing if we use them well. In some cases, we still go back home to who we are. Attitude control is needed.

When I am in the training or coaching mode with clients, I've seen a similar type of response. When we are engaged and worked on a topic such as teambuilding or career pathing and professional development, it is natural for the response to be upbeat even though every once in a while someone doesn't move into a positive space. There are those that MUST be miserable and therein in is a problem. But when in close quarters, individuals will be impacted by the influence of the room. Even the serving staff will start walking more upbeat and exhibit more positivity. All of these responses are normal. Yet, at the end of the day, we still go home to… ourselves. We may have had a long and arduous professional/personal journey with many setbacks. We may not be able to see how it's gonna work out and frankly, we don't think it can. We may be a product of negative talk from our past and our very hearts are dampened by not just the sticks and stones, but also the names that the old children's rhyme told us would not hurt. But they did.

It is the person that you go home with that I want to talk to right now. It is in the midst of all of what we carry that we MUST understand that our attitude will indeed determine our altitude.

In the marketplace, we hear about that "glass ceiling" all the time, which refers to the limitations that are placed on people. The invisible ceiling that looms over the world of emerging professionals, who when they try to go to the next level, crack their heads on the glass ceiling because they didn't see it. That glass ceiling comes in many forms such as gender, age, and racial prejudices/inequities. Those who don't realize it's there may continue to struggle along getting more certifications and degrees, going to more networking events and working from 8 to faint to impress the powers who really may not care about our efforts. This, my friends, is REAL and to be well noted.

Yet the glass ceiling, although powerful, has nothing on the "sticky floor". The sticky floor can be equated to the things that are of our own doing, a major component of which is our attitude. Our attitude is one thing that can propel us beyond preplanned obstacles of our society and the marketplace.

There are so many examples of people who leveraged their ability to believe who they were and the power of who they wanted to be. This first offering of Doses of Career Triage can't even begin to do justice to the list of phenomenal people who have indeed triumphed in the face of being marginalized by those around them. As a reminder, I will list a few whose stories you already know. Just seeing their names will bring to mind how they persisted and insisted on that which was theirs by right. They attained it not by chance BUT on purpose and with purpose in their hearts and a whole lot of GRIT!

Business

Henry Ford
R. H. Macy
F. W. Woolworth
Soichiro Honda
Akio Morita
Bill Gates
Harland David Sanders
Walt Disney
Warren Buffet

Scientists and Thinkers

Albert Einstein
Charles Darwin
Robert Goddard
Isaac Newton
Socrates
Robert Sternberg

Inventors

Thomas Edison
Orville and Wilbur Wright

Public Figures

Winston Churchill
Abraham Lincoln
Oprah Winfrey
Harry S. Truman
Dick Cheney
Barrack Obama
Nelson Mandela

Hollywood Types

Jerry Seinfeld
Fred Astaire
Sidney Poitier
Jeanne Moreau
Charlie Chaplin
Lucille Ball
Harrison Ford
Marilyn Monroe
Oliver Stone

Writers and Artists

Vincent Van Gogh
Emily Dickinson
Theodor Seuss Giesel
Charles Schultz
Steven Spielberg
Stephen King

Zane Grey
J. K. Rowling
Monet
Jack London
Louisa May Alcott

Musicians

Wolfgang Amadeus Mozart
Michael Jackson
Elvis Presley
Igor Stravinsky
The Beatles
Ludwig van Beethoven
Miles Davis

Athletes

Michael Jordan
Stan Smith
Babe Ruth
Tom Landry
Husan Bolt
Serena Williams
Venus Williams
Billy Jean King

Janice's adds

Les Brown
Tyler Perry
Tony Robbins
Robert Kiyosaki
Lisa Nichols

(List adapted from www.quora.com)

There are many more that could be mentioned here. You know it. When you feel like you can't do what you want to do, Google one of these personalities and refresh your memory. When I did that very thing, I found out more about the person which often surprised me and made me think, "Man. What I'm dealing with is chump change compared to this. Stop complaining. Keep it moving, girl. You got this." AND I DO!

Attitude is often a compilation of the impact of experiences we have had and ascribed to, which are based on what we believe to be true.

Our attitude determines what we think about a thing, what it means to us and what we are going to do about it. There are people who have what we call a positive attitude and everything is always HUNKY DORY. Just perfect and fine. Life is always good. They may truly mean this. Why? Because life has always proven to them that if they stay the course, it will all work out for good. I am sure that you have heard that life is 10% of what happens to you and 90% of what you do with what happens to you. Therefore, my personal belief and faith are in this vein.

Early in my professional career, I worked for a property and casualty insurance company in Philadelphia, PA. They were my first employer in the Information Technology industry and I enjoyed the newest of this different life. At least in my eyes, everyone was fairly nice. One rainy Monday morning, a bunch of us crowded into an elevator and headed up. There was some chatter until this one guy jumped in at the last minute before the doors closed. He greeted everyone and started making his rounds. "Ah, man. I can't stand raining days, especially on a Monday." The elevator stopped and few people got off. Then this guy turned to the other side, "Yea… It just makes the day go so slow." The next stop came and a person or two got off. He gave his story left and right for 6 floors. And then when the doors closed, he turned and saw me standing in the back alone, he said, "Umph. Never mind. You're always happy." Exactly!

My life experience, especially now, has shown me that it's all going to be alright! He could not have said anything to me to prove otherwise. Frankly, seeing a Monday morning rain or shine is a straight-up unadulterated blessing. I'm not trying to miss one of those Mondays My attitude is one of GRATITUDE.

When you are facing the challenges of your work environment or the fact that you are out of a job altogether, remember that your attitude about yourself, life, your work situation, your coworkers and your employer has a definite impact on your experience. The laws of nature as explained by Sir Isaac Newton state for every action there is an equal and opposite reaction. You can take that to the bank!

If you are energetic and excited about what's happening even if it's not perfect, chances are you are experiencing a greater amount of satisfaction simply because what you have determined is going to be your norm. If you roll like this, you will see things happen in a way that can only show ultimately on the PLUS side for you. But if your attitude is negative and a downer, even privately, you will see that things around will tend to move in that vein. It's the law. For EVERY action there is an equal and opposite reaction.

✓   Check up

On a scale from 0 to 10, where do you rate your attitude? Zero being very poor and disempowering and ten being powerful and contagious. _____

 Prescription

Spend time every morning, before you engage the world, deciding what the day is going to be like. Identify five components of your attitude where you will set your "thermostat". List them in your hardcopy/digital journal or notebook. An example might be that you write:

- I am CONFIDENT
- I am FUNNY
- I am FOCUSED
- I am DELIBERATE
- I am LOVING

Spend time focusing on them. If you meditate, do that. If you pray, do that. If you do both, you are going to be even more awesomer than the next guy/girl. Make this a practice. It will help you to *calibrate* yourself into a more in-control professional whose outcomes are most predictable according to *plan*. "Meh" is a new word but don't let it be a part of your life. You are headed toward more greatness than ever.

Starting now.

Cowards die a thousand deaths. But the brave only die once.
— Ernest Hemingway

Dose 2

Bravery

What a powerful visual if you can see this in your mind's eye. My encouragement to you is to be BRAVE. It is very easy to settle back in our careers and become complacent after a day, a few months or a lot of years. With several paychecks in, we could be trapped and slowly, our bravery or courage that caused us to land this new career or job eventually goes away. We can find ourselves settling for anything that happens because the fire we had could be gone.

You could be saying, "What fire? I needed a job for real. I took what came along." This chapter is especially for YOU.

In my years in the workplace as a professional and as one who helps corporations and professionals to excel, I see time and time again people who demonstrate the bravery needed to move through the ranks and go to extraordinary heights because they were brave in taking bold steps. Looking at it, they might not call it bravery. But looking back on it, I call it bravery.

I am reminded of a dear friend of mine, Eloise Young, who tells her story as a young professional seeking to find a job where she could settle down, work and get tuition reimbursement so she could attend college. And that she did. She worked and went to Temple University during the day to attain her BS in Computer Science. She proved herself to be an excellent professional and through several different opportunities coming her way, she caught the right rungs as they came by. Unknowingly but with a heart of courage, 30 plus years later, came the emergence of SVP of Technology and Strategic Planning for the Philadelphia Gas Works, which is the largest natural energy provider in the country.

How can I explain Eloise's awesome story in such brevity? It wasn't an easy feat to achieve. You can get the content of her story from her directly<smiles>. But at this point, I will leave you with the impact. The bravery of this young African American woman entering a predominantly male industry and putting down her stakes and marking her territory for the success that would follow her was extremely remarkable. She is a phenomenal example of being brave "in the face of". In the face of what? Whatever it is. Our careers are a direct reflection of the sum total of everything in this book and even more. It is also very much a reflection of the courage and BRAVERY that it would take to do WHATEVER it takes and INSPITE of whosoever poses a threat to us. You know the threats: history, finances, relationships, education, skillset, ethnicity, gender, belief system and so on. These threats can stop or they can make us get it together and DO what needs to be done.

We must be BRAVE.

Your professional and personal life depends on it. The coward says that the marketplace is bad and that there are no jobs out there. The brave person says that it's time to go back to school or revisit/revise my resume. The coward would get scared because they are cutting overtime which is going to impact their paycheck. The brave person says, "I'd better increase my value so that I can increase my income." These are just two totally different ways of approaching the same situation.

A cowardly individual will look for others to take the heavy for moving them along in their career. The brave person, like the firefighter, will run into the situation with the stance that it's game on.

Bravery will get you everywhere you need to be. So, add BRAVERY to your list of prescriptions but don't leave the career triage station before you receive the total diagnosis. You still need to be equipped with other things to help you on this journey to complete health in your career.

It takes bravery to move along on your professional journey, especially when there may not be others in your world who are doing the same thing. I attended the Philadelphia High School for Girls which was outside of my neighborhood. I received negative comments from friends about going to *that* school. This went on for the entire time, I traveled on public transportation for four years to receive the best education Philadelphia had to offer. I and my yellow school jacket traversed rain, snow, wind, and heat. Even though I didn't know what it all meant then, now I know it was indeed bravery/courage on my part to stand out of the crowd. This school had a powerful impact on the lives of all of us who are of that great sisterhood as a Girls' High girl.

Why is bravery important to you as a professional and to your career? Society is truly built on conformity. Sameness. Everyone needs to have people to like them so they can feel they belong as well. Conformity at some level is important, but BRAVERY is what transformation and change are made from. It is truly what makes the world go around. Conformity is for comfort and we all need that. But BRAVERY and the people who demonstrate it and "live out loud" are the people who introduce progress into what would have been a dull and stagnant existence.

Think about the Wright Brothers, Elon Musk, Walt Disney, Catherine Johnson. The BRAVERY it took to follow through on their dreams and hunches catapulted the world into whole new dimensions.

Here's one disclaimer I must make; when you perform acts of bravery like starting a new business, going back to school, I will not consign to the expense of it but I would appreciate being included in the joy and excessive jubilation of the completion of your accomplishments. Fair? <smiles>

✓ Check up

On a scale from 1 to 5, how's your brave-o-meter? One being that you live within everyone's parameters and WILL NOT interrupt the status. Five being, you'll take on the world in a heartbeat. _____

R̽ Prescription

You do not have to be Rambo, however; we do want you to feel empowered to be a self-advocate. Access your current situation of the following:

- Career
- Finances
- Relationships
- Education

- Goal Setting/Achieving
- Life Planning
- _____ (any that I missed?)

Of these, are there any that you believe you need to be more on top of and in control? Do you have a high level of comfort that you are where you want/need to be in this stage of your life? If you answered, "No, I'm cool on all fronts." AWESOME! If there are any that give you less than a confident feeling, maybe it's time to be BRAVE and make the time to get at it. Start your plan:

- Take the list above and prioritize each item focus on #1
- Create a SMART goal to achieve balance and satisfaction for that item
- Put in place all of the resources that you need to help you bring this item in line. This could entail a lot of things like taking a class, engaging professionals for work needed, upsizing/downsizing living quarters. Whatever it seems to be. Do that!
- Determine the best way to keep yourself accountable. Most people need another person for this
- Celebrate major milestones and small wins

Be BRAVE and go after what you want. Now's the time.

Communication is a skill that you can learn. It's like riding a bicycle or typing. If you're willing to work at it, you can rapidly improve the quality of every part of your life. — Brian Tracy

Dose 3

Communications

This is absolutely one of my favorite topics same as the other topics in this book.

John C. Maxwell wrote a book entitled Everyone Communicates, Few Connect: What the Most Effective People Do Differently Everyone Communicates, Few Connect: What the Most Effective People Do Differently, the title alone is so powerful, but I hope you get the picture. Communication has less to do with words and more to do with the conveyance of meaning. There are various ways we can communicate and they include verbal, non-verbal and written. If these were truly the means by which we communicate, I think the world would be a happier and better place. I have taught for many years a principle of communications called the Communications Triangle, as shown here:

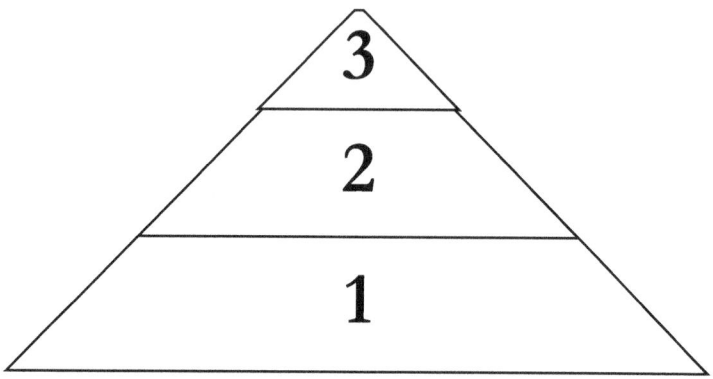

Level 1 is the level where we communicate based on the language we speak whether that is English, Mandarin, Spanish, American Sign Language. I called it the Linguist level. If you and I are speaking English, it simply means we are connecting on Level One of the Communication Triangle. Level 2 is the trickiest of all the levels. This is the level of Understanding.

Do you remember Rush Hour I? My favorite scene was when Jackie Chan and Chris Tucker had this interchange, "Do you understand the words that are coming out of my mouth?" Response. All together now... "Nobody understands the words that are coming out of your mouth." No truer words were spoken in the movie. At that point, they were connected on Level 1 since both were speaking English. They faltered at Level 2, which is understanding. Better yet, comprehension. When communicating with others, it's not always what's being said but how it's being heard. Do I truly UNDERSTAND the words that are coming out of your mouth? Do I get the background or INTENTION of the words or do I only know the IMPACT of the words? If the latter is true therein is the opportunity for all types of misinterpretation and problems to occur. I am convinced that many life issues hinge on our inability to scale Level 2 of this triangle. You can then imagine how impossible Level 3 will be. If we are not speaking the same language, then, of course, we can't go from Level 1 to Level 2 Communications. If we cannot successfully traverse and conquer Level 2, Level 3 will definitely become an IMPOSSIBLE task. That's right. Say IMPOSSIBLE. Level Three is the level of action and outcomes. So, if I don't understand the words that are coming out of your mouth, believe me when I tell you, I will not be able to ACCOMPLISH the desired outcomes. The report will not be right nor will it be on-time. AGAIN. I'm saying, "I'm sorry," because I didn't get it that this was so important to you. There's no way to win here. We must conquer Level 2 Communications.

One great way to get to Level 2 is to follow the advice of Stephen Covey which is to seek to understand and then to be understood which is habit 5 of his 7 Habits of Highly Effective People. As a professional developing great skill for a vibrant career, it would serve you well to master this. We must learn people. An EMOTIONALLY INTELLIGENT person will innately identify another person's motivations, strengths, likes/dislikes and the "what makes them tick". They will seek to understand them. This helps to break down the barriers around Level 2.

Barriers? Yes. Those things that can get in the way of us understanding each other. Things like:

- Educational Level
- Gender
- Age
- Ethnicity
- Corporate Position
- Income
- Industry Jargon
- Past Experiences
- More…

These things make us who we are but they can block us from seeing someone else's point of view OR keep us from being open to listening to them. If you are a "line worker" you may have a thing about "BOSSES". You can't stand them. It's an *authority* issue. So every time a "BOSS" says something to you, you start with a negative attitude. That's a problem. Just because you had a problem with other bosses doesn't make every boss is bad. This is the LEVEL 2 breakdown. How can a "BOSS" get past this? I would personally build a good working relationship showing that I care. The barrier may not come down over night but it's a start. We have to chip away at Level 2 barrier so we can hit Level 3 which is Appreciation and getting the desired outcome of the communication.

Understanding the Communication Triangle can save us a lot of heartache. I have seen people have a "REVELATION" in the middle of this explanation. It's a game changer.

✓   Check up

Regarding your work world, on a scale from 0 to 10, where are you in your consistent satisfaction regarding how you communicate in that environment. Zero being that you don't get them and they don't get you – frustration. Ten being, you all are kicking it on all cylinders – elated. _____

R͟x Prescription

Focus first on the person(s) whose communications with you is the most important in your work environment and work on others as you gain more levels of proficiency. Consider the following if your communications are:

- Productive
- Engaging
- Pleasant
- Fun
- Challenging
- Tense
- Unproductive

If you have great interactions with this person, this is to be celebrated. Connect with them real quick letting them know how wonderful it is to work with them and that you are happy to be associated with them. This is GRATITUDE. They may be shocked but they will return the sentiment.

If your communications are less than positive, consider the communications triangle. Always looking at yourself first, think about what the challenge might stem from.

What could be the breakdown between Level 1 and Level 2?

Even if you feel that you are not at fault in the situation, let's be EMOTIONALLY INTELLIGENT.

Consider what you might do to improve your overall communications with this person.

Now make a careful plan to move toward better communications with this person. After your success, move to the next person. Hopefully, this is NOT a long list. ☺

If you can't fly, run. If you can't run, walk. If you can't walk, crawl. but whatever you do you have to keep moving forward." – Rev. Dr. Martin Luther King

Dose 4

Determination

There have been many times I had set out to do something in my life and allowed myself to be sidetracked. I usually say, "allowed myself" because many of the things that enter into our lives are there by our own permission. There are some things we can't avoid no matter what BUT a large number of so-called interruptions are present because we did not back them down.

I cannot tell you how many times it has happened to me. I would set out on one journey or another only to be waylaid by STUFF. How can that be? No not me, you may say. But I say YES! You! AND ME!

Determination is that thing that will pull us through the muck of distractions and the things we tell ourselves in order to ease the pain of non-completion! We can use any word we want to describe it but the bottom line is that when we set out to do something; complete a certification, network, finish a project on time or learn how to be more organized, it is our determination that will take us to the successful completion of the task at hand.

I have always likened myself to running water… If you dam me up one way, I AM going to come back in another way. For sure, I have "hung my hat" on that many times more in these last years than ever before. I have always rested on my smartness to make a difference in what I have been able to accomplish. Yes, smarts are important. You probably know many smart people who just never make the grade. Pun intended <smiles>. These are the people who know the "HOW" of a lot of things. Yet, somehow their outcomes never go full tilt. They fall short. They push as far as their smartness allows but then not over the top. They can/will/do run out of the energy needed when a few obstacles get in their way. If it gets a little too hard and the challenges become too many and/or frequent, their determination tends to shift and then enough reasonable explanations come along in their minds that makes it easy for them to go on to the next adventure.

Let's talk about what determination means. Webster, my favorite starting place indicates that determination means "firmness of purpose; resoluteness".

Grit is a new term that comes to mind when I think about determination. It entails bearing down on that thing that you have set out to accomplish and saying in your heart that by "any means necessary", as stated by Denzel Washington in the movie Malcolm X, I will make it through this.

Being determined can mean that when hard times come and they do, you as the professional, may have to put something on hold and then come back around to it. But you should always have it in your heart to finish what you start. For example, it seemed like it took me FOREVER to complete my bachelor's degree. I started this journey as most people do, right out of high school. Two years into my college career, I became pregnant with my eldest son. I left the college world to handle this unexpected occurrence in my life. That meant that the first thing I needed to do was to obtain a job.

My first day back home with this new life I learned to live, one of my neighbors, a girl several years older than me, offered some sage advice based on her own experience. She told me that for my age, 19, there were no jobs and that I should go to the welfare office that next Monday and sign up for a check. I asked her how much they gave her per week. She proudly announced $78.00 and food stamps. That did not appeal to me AT ALL. Instead of going to the welfare office on Monday, I took the bus in the other direction to Center City. And I did this for several days. On Friday of that same week, I proudly knocked on her door and announced that I had two jobs: mine and hers. I had garnered employment at a large bank as a teller and at a department store as a sales associate as we call it now. I was determined to not fall into the preset trap that could have sucked me up. I went on to have my son, Michael, and forged my way into the life I had set my heart to achieve.

I did not finish my Bachelors of Christian Ministry degree until after I had my two more children, Stephanie and Daniel and several jobs. But I did it. Was it easy? At that time, NO! I had more responsibility and life to handle than I did when I was 19. But there was a determination in my heart to have a bachelor's degree. Now I am in the process of pursuing my Master's degree. You may say, "Um, Janice… Why now?" I would say, "Um, why not?"

Forge ahead and be determined to accomplish what you set out to do. It may take some planning. As a matter of fact, it *will* take some planning. If you don't plan it, it will definitely be harder to do because you will find yourself falling into *this or that* along the way, and maybe one day, "Wala", you may get there. Planning is important but execution is KING.

Execution is KING. (This book may begin to sound like *True Confessions of a Successful Career Coach*. But hey! I can only give you what I've got. And that is EXPERIENCE). I am one of the best planners you will ever meet. However, I have learned that what fuels determination is execution. Please remember that. EXECUTION.

Execution takes BRAVERY and just straight up GUTS/GRITS. This is because execution can be hard, and no one likes to do the hard things especially when they are not used to doing it. Doing little things? Most of the world can accomplish those. But what it takes to make education into a job and job into a career and a career into something you can love is called EXECUTION.

Those who like to put statistics out have been saying that in the 21st century many professionals can have up to seven different careers over their lifetime in this new marketplace. However, the U.S. Bureau of Labor and Statistics (BLS) has not been so eager to throw a number out there on this one. In a Wall Street Journal article written by Carl Bialik, Seven Careers in a Lifetime? He stated that the BLS posted a corrective note on their website that "no consensus has emerged on what constitutes a career change".

We do know, ladies and gentlemen, that there is no longer the one-job-til-retirement as of old. Not at all. SEVEN different careers is what some of us might just have to face. If you don't get the 26 Doses and MORE under your belt, you will not be able to traverse the marketplace successfully and have a life that is satisfying and fulfilling.

Once you have decided what you are going to set your heart on doing (the goal), you must become determined to make it a reality. Then convert that into a SMART goal which means being Specific, Measurable, Attainable, Realistic and Time-Bound. The GRIT to do what needs to be done is what's going to take you there. We have to act. Execution is really KING.

Right here is where we need to add accountability into our mix. Accountability is always wonderful but I have found that it is a rare person who is able to hold their own feet to the fire. Get that visual. It is not that that person doesn't exist but I know from my own personal experience that accountability of some sort would be beneficial for many. What does that look like? Well, you know me. Right? A coach. A mentor. A teacher. Connect with someone who is empathic but will not take a pathetic excuse. Someone who is encouraging and can push you beyond what you can ever imagine. Do not make it easy for yourself because that is what most will do and then wonder why they have not gotten as far as they could have in a given time frame. Please, execute all you have set your mind to achieve. It beats the alternative. Don't worry about failure. Failure will certainly happen at some point. If a person says they have never failed at anything, then that person has never tried anything. Here is a shortlist of failures to help you gain perspective:

Abraham Lincoln
Wilbur and Orville Wright
Albert Einstein
Sylvester Stallone
Janice Coleman
(**Your name right here**)

Be determined in your own mind and then set out to execute the plan you have made. As you go along, you will have to fine-tune, but never stop your efforts to bring about a great result.

✓   Check up

On a scale from 0 to 10, how determined are you? Zero being a person that hardly ever starts anything toward their goals at all. Ten being the person who finishes everything they start even when OBSTACLES come their way. _____

 Prescription

If you always push through and finish what you start, you are to be applauded because that is an accomplishment!!!

If you find that you are mid-scale 7-9, you may need a little accountability support such as a friend or mentor to help you keep the FIRE going. You can do this!!!

If you are not executing, and the follow up and follow through slips through your fingers, know that you are not alone. Here are a few things to incorporate into these next stages of your life:

- Start with the "WHY". Maybe the goals and desires that you are moving toward are not really ones that are a part of who you are becoming. Therefore, you are losing the drive because it is not true to who you are. Let them go. If they are to be, they will come back around when you are ready.

- Consider if you are READY for the goal that you are thinking about. You might be ahead of yourself and there are more foundational goals to be had. Stop, put it on the shelf and come back to it later with fresh eyes.

Get down to business. Clear everything that might be a distraction and DO THE WORK. Incorporate an accountability partner and set your SMART goal. Keep your PURPOSE and REASONS before you. They will be your anchor when it's hard.

Be BRAVE!

Live as if you were to die tomorrow. Learn as if you were to live forever. – Mahatma Gandhi

Dose 5

Education

Learning is a huge component to anyone's success. That being said, I do not believe that a person must have a multitude of degrees to be a success, but one must be educated in their area(s) of expertise in order to create a strong platform for their success to be a reality.

If you are reading this right now and you know that you want to be the best in your field and go to the next level in your industry, you might have to go back to school. But wait until you are finished with this book in its entirety, and then go online and start researching to find that next school or course to enroll in. <smiles> It is important that you do that.

According to Industry Tap, an online news portal, now information doubles every 12 months soon to be every 12 hours:

> Buckminster Fuller created the "Knowledge Doubling Curve"; he noticed that until 1900 human knowledge doubled approximately every century. By the end of World War II knowledge was doubling every 25 years. Today

> things are not as simple as different types of knowledge have different rates of growth. For example, nanotechnology knowledge is doubling every two years and clinical knowledge every 18 months. But on average human knowledge is doubling every 13 months. According to IBM, the build out of the "internet of things" will lead to the doubling of knowledge every 12 hours. (www.industrytap.com/knowledge-doubling-every-12-months-soon-to-be-every-12-hours/3950)

How often does a new cell phone emerge? It has new capabilities and by the time you learn its new features, a new release drops. Get ready. It's happening right now.

When the 1st iPhone was released, Steve Jobs knew that he was getting ready to change the world and he did. With that change came apps to accompany the phone and its capabilities. How did we ever live without them? We did. But now, we can never go back.

In my daily support of clients, I see that it is almost impossible for professionals to stay abreast of everything that is happening in the marketplaces and their fields of endeavor. This speaks to their RELEVANCE and it can be frustrating. Understandably, when we, the professional, spend much of our time getting ready for work, going to work, being at work and then going home from work, how can we be expected to stay as current as we need to be? That's a hard question. But the reality is, we need to try. If we don't, we can find ourselves to be severely unemployable.

What does unemployable mean? In the context of this book, it does not mean that you can't get a job. Even worse, many of us can find some type of job that will pay us a livable wage. Yet, I dare say that people want to find a job that is challenging and that makes them feel alive when we think about it.

Unfortunately, for many that may not be the case. This unemployability I am referring to is what happens when a professional has missed the gap at the changing of the guards of their industry. We can have awesome skills and NOBODY will need them or pay for them.

When I started in the professional world, I was in Information Technology. This was back in the days of card readers and signing up to use the "terminals" to create/change/maintain program code. Yes, green bar paper, for those who are right now laughing at me. But this is the truth. For four years, I worked for an insurance company and was promoted every year because of my skills and expertise. In the fourth year, my supervisor told me that my next step of promotion should be in a managerial role. This meant that my technical skills would go dormant, at least in my eyes. As you know, IT is a very dynamic industry and everchanging. When he told me this, I decided to look in the NEWSPAPER. I noticed that my skillset was scantly represented in the jobs that were listed in those want ads. That was alarming to me. How could that be? I was only 4 years into this industry and I was already almost OUT!

I decided that I needed to get more training and find a company that was using newer technologies because the future was upon me. And I did just that. Still, over the next six years, the technologies continued to move and there was no stopping it in sight. To this day, IT continues to move ahead at lightning speed. I ultimately did move into a less technical role with my next step being out of IT altogether.

A friend of mine, Beth, who also saw where IT was headed, took it upon herself to attain the requisite training. She postured herself for the movement of the technology in her company and was poised for a HUGE shift that left a lot of her colleagues with antiquated skills and no professional safety net. Many were laid off. The company migrated to new systems and only a few people were able to jump the gap. My friend, Beth, was one of them. Today, she is still viable in IT because she has always looked ahead and positioned herself.

Education and training are essential.

In technology, the model below represents a change in just the last 20 years. A study by Deloitte Consulting in 2017 shows the transition from basic e-learning/blended methodologies have given way to intelligent "machine-driven" platform. This of course we know exponentiates access to information. In my opinion the jury is still out as to whether or not these types of learning platforms can provide a solid foundation for the transitional learning needs of ALL generations. Nonetheless, it is hitting us at "blindingly fast" speeds.

In the good ole days, many corporations had tuition reimbursement opportunities. Some companies still do. If you are in a place where that is true, I hope you are taking advantage of it. The contributions may be taxable which may be challenging. Think of the tradeoff. No education at no risk/no reward. Is that hard to choose?

I have worked with professionals who spent five to ten years at corporations that did offer some training and education opportunities. Some absolutely free! However, one of my clients had not taken advantage of what was made available. Nothing to be added to the Professional Development portion of the resume? Let it not be so! Get the education and training that is available to you.

I am a big proponent of high-value online training. In an occasion with one of my executive coaching clients, I was discussing learning options, I suggested that he look into some resources, one of which was **www.lynda.com** which is an arm of LinkedIn. He checked it out and came back to me with his findings. And what a find! **www.lynda.com** has a reciprocal program through the Philadelphia Free Library, and if you are a cardholder with the library, you can access Lynda and take courses for FREE. Amazing. If it's free, it's for me. He has signed up for many courses since. I shared this information with a family member and she was able to help here company save several thousand dollars a year in training costs.

Education does not have to cost an arm and two legs. That's right, I said two! Regardless, you'd better get some.

How do you know what you should pursue? That depends on the industry that you are in AND what your goals might be right now. Here are some ideas of places to start:

Watch marketplace news channels like CNBC, CNN, CSPAN to get a sense of what types of things are happening in the world. Consider how these things might be impacting the industry you are in; your type of work; and the skillsets that might be needed.

Read news feeds like FLIPBOARD, LinkedIn, USA TODAY, Bloomberg to name a few. There, you can catch a glimpse of what's trending in the world and what companies are doing.

Identify some progressive people where you currently work and watch what they do. If possible be BRAVE and ask them for an informational meeting. This type of meeting is not an interview but an opportunity for discovery regarding your interest and what's currently going on in the marketplace. Determine if they are a good candidate for MENTORSHIP. That's a next-step action for the future.

Look at the New York Times Best Seller List of Business books (June 2019):

01. DARE TO LEAD by Brené Brown
02. BAD BLOOD by John Carreyrou
03. ATOMIC HABITS by James Clear
04. I WILL TEACH YOU TO BE RICH, 2nd Edition by Ramit Sethi
05. THE LATTE FACTOR by David Bach and John David Mann
06. WOLFPACK by Abby Wambach
07. TRILLION DOLLAR COACH by Eric Schmidt, Jonathan Rosenberg and Alan Eagle
08. PRINCIPLES by Ray Dalio
09. EXTREME OWNERSHIP by Jocko Willink and Leif Babin
10. GRIT by Angela Duckworth

Pick one of the Top Ten and read it. Yes, read it. I am a hardcopy book person myself. Once in a while, I make it through an online book. But by and large, I like the tactile feel of the hardcopy. I know you have heard that leaders are readers. Statistics show that most people will not even read one book in a year's time. You could not even want to be average because you are reading *this* book. Find a book and read it.

My personal list of favorite business books includes:

The Bible (King James Version)
Top Performance, Zig Ziglar
See You at the TOP, Zig Ziglar
Think and Grow Rich, Napoleon Hill
10 Life Lessons, Dr. Phil Staff
The Wealth Choice, Dr. Dennis Kimbro
7 Habits of Highly Effective People, Stephen Covey
21 Irrefutable Laws of Leadership, John C. Maxwell
What Color is Your Parachute?, Richard Bolles
Good to Great, Jim Collins
5 Levels of Leadership, John C. Maxwell
The Richest Man in Babylon, George Samuel Clayson

10X Rule, Grant Cardone
Rich Dad, Poor Dad, Robert Kiyosaki
Becoming, Michelle Obama
Money: Master the Game, Tony Robbins
Awakening the Giant Within, Tony Robbins
How to Win Friends and Influence People, Dale Carnegie

All of this to find trends? Yes. It can help you in your search to expand and/or determine the need to change your career. In his article, *Seven Ways to Identify and Evolve with Industry Trends* (www.inc.com June 5, 2019), John Hall concurs that finding and following business trends helps protect a professional against the potential of lagging behind those who make it happen in the marketplace. He gave straight forward ways to accomplish this:

> 1. Take advantage of industry research and trends reports.
> 2. Regularly follow publications and influencers in your industry.
> 3. Use different tools and analytics systems to identify the direction trends are heading.
> 4. Make it a point to surround yourself with smart people.
> 5. Build and maintain a close group of advisers.
> 6. Ask the right questions and listen to your customers.
> 7. Learn to accept--and even embrace--change.

For some trades and industries, this type of in-depth activity will make a lot of sense. I will say that you can't go wrong with this approach though.

If you begin a practice of this, you will start to identify what will be fit for you to pursue. Then follow that path. Begin to carry out more specific research, which may include visiting a university where they can aid with assessments and other tools. There are also online tools like SkillsFinders™ where you can identify your prominent skills sets and begin to match them with today's marketplace needs and trends. There is a lot you can do. I want you to do something.

Your pursuit of education and training can land you in some great places and maybe some awkward places. But remember that it is only your DETERMINATION that will shine that light on the next steps for you. Even if the education you decide to follow does not move you out of your current job/career but only fortifies your expertise, it will certainly be time well-spent.

✓ Check up

Consider where you are in your current career and/or what you know about the career that you want. On a scale of 0 to 10, where do you fall with the required information about what knowledge you need to have? Zero being that you are not current enough in the industry to know what a professional in your career should know in today's marketplace. Ten being that you have full knowledge of the current educational requirements needed for your career/ you have them and/or know where to start to get them. _____

℞ Prescription

Here's where research comes into play. Let's get started!

1. Reach out to someone who you believe is in the know about what's happening the marketplace. Meet with them to discuss what you are currently doing and what you may be thinking about. Or that you don't have any current direction but want to have open dialogue about

the marketplace as you are exploring for your next steps.

2. Explore your current employer's website for insight into what they are doing. Follow your instincts regarding possibilities.

3. Investigate/visit/join an industry association.

Which will you do? _____ When will you start? _____

Whenever you want to achieve something, keep your eyes open, concentrate and make sure you know exactly what it is you want. No one can hit their target with their eyes closed. — Paulo Coelho, The Devil and Miss Prym

Dose 6

FOCUS

In my program, Are You HYPED? (Harnessing Your Potential Every Day), FOCUS is the main highlight and ingredient for a person be able to harness the potential that is inside of them.

When I think of the power of FOCUS, I am reminded of the power of electricity. It is one of the most widely used energy sources in the world. So many industries have used this energy to cause the world to progress.. Now it is unfathomable that we could ever have been without it. According to ThoughtsCo.com, the timeline of electricity goes back as far as 600 B.C. with references to what is now called static electricity. The use of electricity has expanded beyond what I strongly believe scientific pioneers like Benjamin Franklin could ever comprehend. We are still advancing on these developments every day.

Consider the utility of electricity with regard to light. The incandescent lightbulb uses the power of electricity to give soft light to a room. This lightbulb may emit a low-grade heat that is negligible to the comfort of even the coolest of rooms at 70° F. This is electricity in its most common form found in nearly every household or building on the planet. This is done usually without incident.

We can take that same source of energy, electricity, and spiral it through a series of circuits which concentrates its power into a laser, such as can be used to cut through a steel plate and anything else in its path. I would not want anyone to attempt to put their hand anywhere near that. This is because, unlike the warmth of the incandescent light, the velocity of the electricity emitting from that laser is not going to be negligible upon contact with that hand.

The difference between the lightbulb AND the laser is not the type of energy used, but the concentration of that same energy!

In like manner, it is the same power we can garner when we implement this FOCUS into our daily lives. When we FOCUS, we bring into existence the effects of what I call critical mass. It's simply momentum. In my personal experience, I have helped many professionals realize this over the years.

One of the things most career coaches I know suggests is that we must create a TARGET COMPANY list. These might be the top ten to twenty companies that are of interest to us. This does one major thing for the job seeker; it brings FOCUS. It is this action alone that can help the job seeker to put the blinders on and create so much power in their job search as they begin to traverse the marketplace. Don't be afraid. This will not cut you off from other opportunities. I will show as we go along.

Along with the target companies list, you should develop a list of your preferences regarding a job which includes desired salary, company size, location, etc. You can then begin to pursue the companies by doing research, going to their websites (applying for an open position), reaching out to people that you know who have some link to that company (either working there, having worked there in the past and so forth). You will begin to see patterns and of course, you will get ideas. You will start to make connections that can lead you to opportunities. You may even expand your list or reduce your list because of what you have learned. If you are diligent, you will begin to go in a direction that will yield the outcome you want.

Everybody's story is different.

A gentleman I worked with in 2008 during the big marketplace upheaval had a unique experience. Contrary to what I would ever suggest for anyone, he had one particular employer that he wanted to work for. He had been laid off and was in a very competitive industry; Financial Services, specifically Credit Card Management. He picked out a company that appealed to him and he was DETERMINED that this was the right company for him. Ummm. I thought. Let's not be SO FOCUSED, even though, I believe it works. But here, he was DETERMINED. He set his sights on that company and it was a go for him. Neither he nor I knew anyone in that company. At that time, the use of LinkedIn was not so prolific, but we did our best. He came up with a strategy and began to move forward with it. He was very persistent and soon identified/connected with a person inside this company who was willing to give him an informational meeting with no strings attached. Several weeks later, this meeting yielded an interview for a position which he was well-qualified. He progressed through the interview process and received an offer. Before the virtual ink was dry on the offer, the offer was rescinded because the position was eliminated. Yes, that's what was happening in the downturn in 2008/2009. Back to square one? No. They liked him and added him to the run for a similar position! And he received an offer. Whew! No wait! That position was eliminated. He stayed FOCUSED and motivated. Yet again, he was included in a third lane for another position. He was then in a holding pattern. Challenging? Yes! He had a planned vacation that was upon him. Without an offer, he went away to Germany for two weeks. I told him to watch this unfold and that he'd receive an offer while in the air. And he did. Upon landing in Germany, he received a call with an offer. This would be the one that he accepted and ran into the day after his return from Germany. He has been with that company still to the writing of this chapter of this book.

A HAPPY ENDING!

Don't try this at home, boys and girls. Well, maybe you should. It can be hard on the heartstrings. His DETERMINATION and FOCUS surely paid off in spades.

There is power in our ability to FOCUS on a task, goal or desire and to make it a reality. Of course, there should be a balance in all we do. Radically FOCUSED people have accomplished so many wonderful things that the world has been able to enjoy and benefit from over the years.

✓   Check up

On a scale from 1 to 10 how easily distracted do you find yourself to be with regard to your efforts whether on the job or getting things done toward your professional development? One being when a phone call or a text notification comes along you immediately response, lose track of time and totally forget what you wanted to accomplish and ten being that you are like a dog with a bone and are able to stay to task even when other things squeeze in, you know where you left off and you keep on moving toward the desired end. _____

R̶X̶ Prescription

Focus is a function of your mind and your ability to stay on course. If you do have a hard time staying on a task for any given time or to its completion, let's start with some suggestions from Brian Tracy:

- Plan your day the night before (write it down or keep it in an electronic notes app like EVERNOTE)
- Go OFFLINE. Unplug if you able. Set your phone aside and check it every hour or so
- Start earlier in the morning
- Declutter your workspace and home. Organize your personal world for more efficiency

He says, "There are no shortcuts. To be a big success, start a little earlier, work a little harder and stay a little later."

Also, prioritize your professional goals, work tasks and life goals/responsibilities. Know that certain things have to be done on a daily basis and done well. Things that you are working toward can vie for your attention. Seek to keep them in their place and be like a laser in your attention to them. One month of consistent effort can yield you greater results than a year of dabbling. If you want results, focusing intently will take you where you want to be.

Stay with it!

Give thanks with a grateful heart. Give thanks because of what the Lord has done for us. – Give Thanks by Don Moen and Paul Wilbur

Dose 7

Gratitude

This term gratitude is being used some much in our society and even more in the marketplace in recent times. It truly deserves its own chapter even though it is an ATTITUDE that we mentioned previously.

Recently, I was fortunate to be included in a program with a regional HR firm as a coaching partner for one of their clients. The program is designed to bring a new component of coaching support and professional development to a select group of employees within the company. Janet, one of the wonderful people I had the opportunity to support gave me as a thank-you, a book entitled The Little Book of Gratitude by Dr. Robert A. Emmons, a leading expert on the effects of gratitude on the brain. She bought it while at a museum she visited as she continues to work on one of her life's passions. I keep this book on my coffee table in my living room. I love the contents of the book, but I cannot include them here. But here's a tidbit:

Inner jacket:

Gratitude gives us the strength of character to make life better not only for ourselves but also for others. In this book, Dr. Robert A Emmons, the world's leading scientific expert on gratitude, sets out simple, proven practices and techniques that will help you grow your gratitude every day.

Back Cover:

Gratitude is the simple, scientifically proven way to increase happiness and encourage greater joy, love, peace, and optimism into our lives.

Through easy practices, such as keeping a daily gratitude journal, writing letters of thanks, and meditating on the good we have received, we can improve our health and wellbeing, enhance our relationships, and heighten feeling of connectedness.

Easily accessible and available to everyone, the practice of gratitude will benefit every area of your life and generate a positive ripple effect.

That's it in a nutshell.

Gratitude is so powerful that it is now a scientific discipline. I find that amazing because it has been proven over the years to be true. From ancient days, the Bible says, "In everything give thanks…" 1 Thessalonians 5:18 and with no scientific theory behind it, but proven. Science now shows that when people have an attitude of gratitude, it impacts their brains in a positive way by releasing stress and enhancing the longevity of life.

Gratitude is powerful.

If you feel like you have nothing to be grateful for, think again.

Seriously. Contemplate on the following:

Zig Ziglar, my favorite speaker of all-time, so experience this:

A woman called his office asking to meet with him when he came to her area for an upcoming speaking engagement. He agreed to do so but he made her understand that he had a short period of time but would be happy to meet with her. They finally met. She proclaimed that the place where she worked was horrible and that she wanted to leave but was stuck there. Zig, being Zig said to her that her speculations were true and that they were actually thinking of firing her. She was shocked at this statement and wanted to hear more. He started to rehearse the problem she had already listed and instructed her to act fast. He asked her if there was anything she liked about her job and told her to make a list of what was good about the job before she eventually loses it. And so she did:

1. Paid every week.
2. Nice place work environment; cool in the summer/warm in the winter.
3. Close to her home.
4. Vacation days.
5. Sick time.
6. Comfortable place to sit to do her work.
7. Money to take care of her life's needs and some desires.
8. Insurance benefits.
9. Lunch breaks.
10. Nice parking lot for her car.

You get the point?

He then went on to tell her to take this list and go back to her home and read the list every morning for 30 days, "I love my job because…". After the 30 days, she reached back out to Zig and said that an amazing thing happened. The people were more pleasant, the boss was nicer and things were so much better.

He told her that they probably were thinking that they'd not fire her. So for this, she was relieved.

Could it be how we see what we see that determines its impact on us? Everything is not always going to be peachy-keen for sure. But what do we see when we look at our circumstances? If we put on the glasses of gratitude, we could get ahead of our own despair. If we put on the glasses of gratitude, we could release the chemicals in our brain in order to help us to cope a little bit better. It might free us of the stuff that holds us back from embracing the good things around us.

The gratitude factor can lift us to an entirely new arena of hope and freedom. Yes, freedom. I have found that being contrary makes me tired. There is a downward spiral that comes along with the bad side of things. Everything rolls down when we get it going.

Be grateful for the things that you have, knowing that it is only going to get better. I heard this in three totally different renditions of The Best is Yet to Come:

- Frank Sinatra (Big Band)

- Grover Washington: Feat. Pattie LaBelle (Jazz)

- Donald Lawrence (Gospel)

Regardless of the style that suits your fancy, the facts remain the same. FOCUS on the beneficial and good parts of where we find ourselves and we can make it out of the turbulence into the more suitable.

You may not be able to change your job situation today. BUT. BUT. BUT. You can change how you see what you see TODAY! TODAY! TODAY!

Make a decision to roll on the side of gratitude and watch your workplace start to "better up" (I just made that up… <smiles>) right now.

✓ Check up

On a scale from 0 to 5, how frustrated are you with the "things" around you or lack thereof? Zero being mild to no frustration, I am at ease. Five being that you can't find a sense of rest in your head about the things going on in "your world" and it doesn't seem to be getting any better.

 Prescription

I think, regardless of where we fall on the scale, we can all use a nice dose of expression of gratitude. Every day take a moment or two to sit and think… List five things for which you are grateful. If you keep a journal, this might go well there.

If you are experiencing major overwhelm about your career/job, you may need to go the route that Zig Ziglar suggested to the woman. Make your list of 10 and review it every day in addition to the nightly gratitude log. We must remind ourselves of how well things are on a regular basis.

Remember that 2/3 of the world live on $2.00 a day.

The greatest health is wealth – Virgil

Dose 8

Health

Here's a dose you may not have been expecting since we are talking about careers. Yet, I believe that it is important to take some time to recognize that health and healthy practices are important to our career.

Some careers can be stressful by nature of the career itself. Other careers can be stressful because of how we handle them or that we are unable to handle them because of our own state of being. If we as individuals do not know how to handle a fast-paced work environment and we find ourselves in a fast-paced work environment, then we're cooked. This can snowball into multiple issues that make us incapable of handling our work well. At this point, we begin to think it's the job, it's the boss, it's the coworkers, when in fact the fault is truly ours.

Maintaining healthy practices can keep us ready for whatever comes our way. What practices might these be? I'm glad you asked:

- Proper sleep
- Proper nutrition
- Proper exercise

- Proper downtime/fun/frolic

In the book, 7 Habits of Highly Effective People, Dr. Stephen Covey refers to the Time Management Matrix in Habit 2 – First Things First. He talked about the balance of life knowing that we really cannot manage time, but that we can only manage how we use the time that we have because time is a fixed number at 168 hours per week. That is the eternal 24 hours in a day. All the things that I listed above are covered in Quadrant 2 of the Time Management Matrix. These are things that are what Covey says are important but not urgent. They don't knock the doors down. But when ignored the doors could literally fall off the hinges. For instance, taking that much needed time to go to lunch while being at work is important. It's a Quadrant 2 activity. Aside from just being a smart thing to do. Not doing so on a regular basis can make you "wound too tight". Check out the movie *Falling Down* starring Michael Douglas. When doing Quadrant 2 activities on a consistent basis for your career and life overall everything else has a better chance of staying even keel.

Why are healthy practices important to sustain your career? It is because you need Life in order to live LIFE.

I know many people who have pushed themselves through life. Living to please others and supporting others in their quests. RESPONDING TO ANSWERING THE REQUEST OF others to their own detriment. They have suffered through sleepless nights with long work hours and poor eating habits only to find out that when they have finished giving their all for the CAUSE, people will move on without them.

Yes. Firing. Yes. Being laid off. Yes. Being overlooked for promotions. That's in the work world. What about the personal landscape where we give our all? Folks might show up at the hospital when you are admitted for some stress-related situation. Maybe. They might be overheard talking about how we were always there for them, but that will not fix any health situation that we might be in because we ran on all cylinders. Having hindsight is 20/20, so let that be the case.

I am hearing now more than ever the phrase selfish but not in the way that may have been used in the past. Selfishness is not positive when it refers to people who ignore the needs of others only to consume their time and resources on themselves in a lavish inordinate way. This is irresponsible. But in more recent years, hearing about selfishness means that a person is more cognizant of their own needs and it ensures that they tend to their own personal state to maintain life's healthy balance. This is important. Maybe 'selfishness' is not the most fitting term. I have also heard it called "extreme self-care". Nonetheless, I hope you know what I mean.

A very common example of this selfishness is when you are on an airplane and the flight attendants go through their presentation. They come to the statement about, "In the case of an emergency, the oxygen masks will drop down. Please, PUT YOURS ON FIRST!" Well now! How selfish can you be? Put the mask on yourself FIRST? But what about the child, the spouse, the elderly? You have to ensure that you can help them and if you do not take care of yourself first, you will not even be around to help them. End of story.

Do the things that are important for your own wellbeing or you will not be around to lavish on others the greatness of who you really are. Point blank. I double "D" dare you to be kind to yourself, above all, then watch how the rest of the world and the rest of your world will fall into their proper perspective in your head and in theirs.

✓ Check up

On a scale of 1 to 10, how do you feel overall? One being run down and discomforted. Ten being excellent. _____

 Prescription

This is not a medical book although we are using medical terminology throughout its pages. Please ensure that if you are not on the upper ends of this scale that you stop yourself in your tracks and get there. There is no career goal that supersedes our need to be in great health. Let's be well from head to toe. This can mean that we need to have our BRAVERY in gear. I feel you on that. Be encouraged that it's all about you right now! Below, make a list of your healthcare professionals. Add more if needed.

- Primary
- Dentist
- OB/GYN
- Podiatrist
- Optometrist
- Nutritionist
-
-
-

If you are not on a regular routine of visiting them, please ask an accountability partner to assist you with scheduling an appointment. If you need a new professional, ask around for referrals.

When will you schedule? _____

There are other aspects of your health to review and take stock of. That includes weight, nutrition, exercise, sleep and fun/relaxation/recreation. Look at your life/lifestyle and get in balance. Living in total health is a great goal. Don't you think?

If your emotional abilities aren't in hand, if you don't have self-awareness, if you are not able to manage your distressing emotions, if you can't have empathy and have effective relationships, then no matter how smart you are, you are not going to get very far. – Daniel Goleman

Dose 9

Intelligences

Have you ever heard of EMOTIONAL INTELLIGENCE? It is a term or discipline that was brought to the forefront in 1995 in a book by Daniel Goleman. It is a powerful tool when understood. It had been powerful over the years, even without the label "EMOTIONAL INTELLIGENCE" and you will see why in this book. Formerly, it was called Mother Wit, social skills, or plain old common sense.

This is alarming:

> Seventy five percent of careers are derailed for reasons related to emotional competencies, including the inability to handle interpersonal problems; unsatisfactory team leadership during times of difficulty or conflict or inability to adapt to change or elicit trust. – Center for Creative Leadership

I bet we all can attest to this as the truth.

There are some people in this world who naturally know and understand how to get along with and deal with people different than themselves, not just racially or because of gender. But people who from their very core are just different from others. They see things differently. They move and breathe differently. These people show up in all different ways in our lives, and if you are in the workforce AND/OR you are a leader as well, YOU WILL HAVE TO DEAL with different types of people.

EMOTIONAL INTELLIGENCE is a key that can help you be successful and strengthen your ability to move your organization forward soundly.

You may be a person who has had an EI assessment done or you've been trained in EI over your professional career. Then, that is awesome. That means that you are more readily able to navigate the turbulence that can occur within your own head when you bump into the situations you can experience when dealing with others. EI is designed to help you become successful, have a greater level of understanding and maintain your own equilibrium. How ingenious. The reason why I say it has been powerful over the years, even without the EI stamp on it, is because for many years, people learned to "count to three" before responding. Or "Just ignore them." Or, "I need a break…" and the like. These coping skills and more show that we were in the process of managing ourselves or our contact with someone else.

Goleman's Five Components of EMOTIONAL INTELLIGENCE are:

❖ Self-awareness – Knowing one's own emotions
❖ Self-regulation – Managing one's own behavior
❖ Internal Motivation – Self Motivation
❖ Empathy – Understanding the emotions of others
❖ Social Skills – Building/Managing Relationships

Why is being emotionally intelligent important in your career front? Because it will help you survive unsure times, unruly workers and incompetent leaders. Being emotionally intelligent will help you stay balanced because things will certainly come after you, or so it may seem. If you are EI, you will see it for what it really is in order to handle it appropriately.

I remember in my IT career, I worked with a woman who became the bane of my existence. Although she was not my direct supervisor, she took it upon herself to always check up on me and my projects. This being early in my career, I did not know to have a talk with anyone like HR or even my manager. So I became frustrated, suffered silently with the poking that I was receiving in this unsettling work relationship. So after a while, I decided to leave the company. People don't often leave companies. People leave people. So, I left and became a consultant and was assigned to work on a project in another state altogether. In my mind, "Now I'm free." Yeah. Right? Ah… No! Lo and behold, there was a woman who worked on this consulting project with me, and for all intents and purposes, it was the SAME woman. She got on my nerves more than the first one. It was then that I had to ask myself a question. "Since these people are mutually exclusive and the only common denominator in this is me, so what is it about me that makes me irritated with the two of them?" I had to become self-aware around this issue in order to become free from it. Now that I am well into my career, even beyond that one, I can navigate these behaviors and NOT be irritated or impacted at all.

Nowadays, some REAL stuff doesn't even get a rise out of me. Some stuff still does. <smiles> Yet, I may not even notice the person or particular ATTITUDE because I am in self-preservation mode keeping myself in check regarding my feelings saving the emotional responses for their proper use at the right times.

There is a proper time for certain emotional responses. And maybe with a heightened sense of urgency. If your systems just went down and Customer Service is at a standstill, it is not the time to decide to go to lunch and let the chips fall where they may because you are being cool, calm, and collected. Not at all. You can maintain your cool but you better move like a bat out of the abyss to get the proper people on the problem right away. You had better stay on it until all systems go, making the right decisions and demonstrating unwavering leadership at that moment. Your not being able to do so would prove disastrous and not EMOTIONALLY INTELLIGENT at all.

I have found that in every work environment, there is a culture. Some you may find will seem to be the same. But nonetheless, they can be different. As a professional, you will more than likely find that you must learn how to navigate these cultures. Doing this well is going to be important to you.

Your ability to be EMOTIONALLY INTELLIGENT and aware of others' INTELLIGENCES as well will give you a definite edge on your career. Also, it will afford you the ability to stand out when interrelating with people. You will have the diplomatic upper hand and others will admire how you are able to handle yourself well in so many situations.

✓   Check up

On a scale from 1 to 5, how familiar are you with your own EMOTIONAL INTELLIGENCE quotient based on the Daniel Goleman's original work. One being you never heard of it before this book to 5 being you know about it and where you fall in every category and maybe even having taken an assessment before. _____

 Prescription

The best suggestion here is to read the book. You will find yourself somewhere in the pages and you will find your way to a better you by the time you are done.

.

If you can't find joy in the path you are on and what you are working toward now, how do you expect to find joy once you get there? – Anonymous

Dose 10

Joy

Joy?

Is this a business book? Yes! Then you may ask why I am using a word like "joy". It goes along with ATTITUDE. Every word has an ATTITUDE associated with it. Now, we are making some radical shifts in who we are as professionals. You almost can't get any more radical than GRATITUDE and JOY!

I once had a coachee push back with regard to a book I suggested she should read. She thought it to be too spiritual in its nature. After all, the author was a Christian as it was indicated in his biographical summary. I assured her that the book was a great book. The author was an authority on the topic and "Yes,' He is a Christian. Why was she alarmed? She said that she was not brought up that way and that she didn't want to read anything that had to do with it although the book was clearly focused on the business topic at hand. I asked her to trust me on this, and she acquiesced. She read the book cover to cover and LOVED the author.

That said! Some words are associated with different disciplines, philosophies, and faiths. That is true. Regardless of that, if the principle of JOY creates a challenge for you right now, you probably really need it! <smiles>

JOY is an inner state that helps us to regulate outer situations which are temporary at best. You may look at someone and say that they are always happy. *That* could be interchanged for JOY in the minds of most people.

I tend to break out into song from time to time because I have learned how to focus on what I want to have happening versus what may be going on around me. Once when I was about 26 years old I was sitting at my desk and I burst out into song. Not loud. But obviously loud enough for the coworker next to me to hear me. She said, "Can you keep that down? You're always singing." I said I'm always happy. She responded with an "umph" and kept working. This same person happened to ALWAYS be on edge and not happy about a thing in life. Not one blessed thing. My singing was not the problem.

I have happiness inside and it pushes its way out on a regular basis. How about you?

I believe that things seem to respond to how you feel. Does that mean that everything will be hunky-dory ALL the time? Probably not. Charles Swindoll has been quoted saying that life is 10% of what happens to you and 90% of how you react to what happens to you.

So why not choose JOY!

You may have read Victor Frankl's book, Man's Search for Meaning. You can't find many situations more challenging than being in a concentration camp with death all around you. He found the strength from within to not see what was happening as stronger than what he felt inside which had to be some level of JOY. This kept him above the situation. Could he smile? NO. Could he sing out loud, Probably not. But JOY or happiness does not require that the outer circumstances allow it to exist. It requires that the person allow the inner state to be in charge.

This refers to Dose One, ATTITUDE. Allow your ATTITUDE to be that of rest and peace. Think that everything is cool and more things will be cool. Think that this is going to be a GREAT day, and a great day it will be, simply because you have put a dose of joy on it.

The Operations Director where I used to work would respond to a "How are you?" with "I've never had a bad day. Some just better than others." What a great way to think!

Slap a dose of JOY on your day. Smile, and smile again. Maybe not too much at first because people may think something is wrong for real. But then, hey, who really cares what they think? Smile. The inside of you will begin to seep out of you.

Why do you think Pharrell Williams song, HAPPY, made the charts at lighting speed? Everybody really does want a reason to be happy. We do. This song gave us a chance to sing out and belt it out for good reason.

There is an innate difference between joy and happiness though. That's why I choose to write about JOY. Joy does not depend on external circumstances.

Put some joy on right now. Consider that of all that could have happened to you. Hopefully you have reasonably great health and a good life that's getting better. Get into a state of JOY about these things.

✓ Check up

On a scale from 0 to 10, what's your joy-o-meter like on a daily basis? Zero being that everything is in the dumps as far as you are concerned, you can't wait to go back to sleep, and you NEED someone else to keep you out of your MOOD to 10 being that you can fuel a space shuttle with some juice to spare.

____

 Prescription

Gather things in your life that make you smile and laugh. There's a lot that can and will go wrong but be more lighthearted in your approach. Watch a funny movie or get a hold of the Three Stooges (my personal favorite). Add good OLD television into your routine. Get a book of corny jokes or ask Google or Siri to make you laugh. Take a hiatus from watching a lot of news especially politics. <smile>

Just don't be SOOOOO serious.

This Dose's cure is an accumulation of several. Combined with GRATITUDE and WORTH.

You will be uplifted in your heart. Watch and see.

You were born to win, but to be a winner, you must plan to win, prepare to win, and expect to win. – Zig Ziglar

Dose 11

Kinetic

It wasn't until I was an adult that I really appreciated what I learned in my Physics class about the Laws of Energy. We all know that there are two types of energy. Potential energy which is energy at rest, and kinetic energy which is energy in motion. This understanding became HUGE in my mind when a note came about my youngest son on one faithful day.

The teacher wrote that he had great potential and continue to encourage him to grow and work hard. In an attempt to explain this to a 7-year old, I had an inspiration. I took a book and placed it on the mantelpiece and told him that potential was like this book resting still on the mantel. Then I pushed the book to allow it to drop to the floor and I explained to him that the book was moving and no longer still or "at rest". It has used energy to get from one place to the other. Right then, a light went on for me.

For many years, I have heard people say about others that they have great potential. I am sure that you've heard that as well. I know that they are well-intentioned in saying so, but here is what I hear now. That the person has a lot they could be doing, and a lot that they can do based on what they know and what they are capable of. To this point, they have yet to accomplish it.

Right? That is POTENTIAL. Energy at rest.

My friends, it is time for us to turn our potential into a reality we can touch! We must now be KINETIC if that makes sense. We must become what we really have inside of us or we are wasting away.

To have great potential at 7 is an awesome thing, but I am heartbroken if that can still be said of me at 60. GREAT POTENTIAL? What's gone wrong? If we are still in the blocks after many years of having potential that is yet to be realized, we need to get moving.

That's right. Get moving!

There are many things that can hold us back. I admit that. That's why you are reading 26 Doses. These various topics and ideas are to push you into a state of KINETICISM. Getting moving!

If you feel that you have been in the state of POTENTIAL for too long, you are probably right. Here's the book, "26 Doses of Career Triage" which has been in the wings for TOO MANY YEARS and FULL of POTENTIAL. You see me in the same boat right here. If I don't get this book out into the world, the next book won't come. And the next. AND the next!

What have I been waiting for?

What are you waiting for?

George Eliot said, "It's never too late to become what you might have been." This is a true statement. Your brain may have immediately started with all the reasons why you can't become what you want to be. Instead, tell your brain, I mean your left brain to back down. Now is your time.

If you are in the lab conducting an experiment on energy, how do you advance an object from one place to another? You move it. There's nothing tricky about that. You have to exert some energy to get an object from one place to the other. This is in layman's terms, of course. Well, it's the same with us.

We must introduce something that is going to get us moving. Hopefully it's not a layoff that helps us to make that much needed employment move. Please don't think that every layoff is that. But let's be proactive which is the 1st Habit in the 7 Habits of Highly Effective People.

How can we be kinetic in a world that is full of potential? By taking action. Everything that we are reviewing in this book will definitely assist you in pulling your brain together around what needs to be done and what can be done to bring your career to a healthy state.

The mark of someone who is in a KINETIC state is that they have this mindset of achieving their goals. NOT that they have them. That's reality. For many years, I carried a lot of goals around in my head and in my heart, but I was not being KINETIC.

Look back over your life. One year. Two years. Five years.

Did you have goals? Did you achieve them? Did you make it to the next?

Doing things just to do them, although trite, is more kinetic than not doing anything at all.

Zig Ziglar said, "I'm not gonna let up, shut up or give up until I'm caught up." He did just that. He courageously spoke to thousands of people well into his 80's. He died at 86 from pneumonia. He retired in 2012 and was kinetic because he chose to be.

Getting into the driver's seat of your life is what being KINETIC is all about. It is easy to expect that an employer will do it. Or, if you are early in your career that your parents will do it. But this cannot be the case. You must light and maintain your own fire. You must do this because it is yours and your responsibility. I want to challenge the overachievers reading this book as well.

Why? Because your 20% effort looks like others' 100%. You can get away with looking like you're kicking it out. Really you're coasting. Who knows? You do. You must set your goals further ahead than most people. Don't break anything but make a real mark on this earth because you have the POTENTIAL to do so.

One thing that will happen as you become more kinetic is that you will end your days feeling a little more depleted and that's a good thing. Why? Because the more you put out or give out, the more room there is for MORE to be produced. So, put it out. It will come back in multiple fashion as well. Guaranteed.

✓   Check up

On a scale from 1 to 10, how do you approach your goals and the things you intend to accomplish? One being "I talk a good game or maybe not that good," and you are always at the same goal every year to ten being, "I get on them quickly using my planning tool to keep myself going until I accomplish what I want to do while making adjustments where necessary." _____

R̲X̲ Prescription

You will need a book or online tool to keep this information in one place. Draw a line in the sand! Whatever is in the past is in the past. This exercise is to gauge where you are so that you know, and then you move to where you want to be.

Spend time considering all of what you want and NEED to do in your life as you see it right now. Write down the goals that you are in process with; evaluate where you are with each of them. Apply the 4 D's of Time Rescue (found in Dose 20). process to them. Now with what's left after the 4 D's, prioritize the goals. Now literally put the start dates of your goals on your calendar setting reminders for 1 month, 1 week and 1 day before. Color code these goals in RED. This can make the red fill up a bit. (If you use Google Calendar this will be easy to do). Do not hesitate to schedule them out as far as it makes sense; 1 month or 1 year. When the date arrives, get started! Easy? Maybe not. But do it anyway. Let's get moving along.

You may want to have an accountability partner who is on fire with life. They can help give you perspective and clarity.

If you want to <u>grow and develop yourself</u>, embrace failure. If you want to become the best at what you do, you've got to be willing to fail, again and again. And then finally, one day, you can fail your way to greatness. — Les Brown

Dose 12

Loss / Lost

One of the realities of spending time working on your career is that there may have been a time when you did not put enough energy into becoming what you wanted to be. Maybe you found yourself on the side of the marketplace where everything always rolled in your favor. That's awesome. This work will fill those crevices that are still to be filled.

On the other hand, if you have been in the workforce for years and have worked extremely hard and found that the marketplace has moved faster than you can keep up and you feel that you have lost ground, no worries, there's still time to achieve all of that. Losing is for losers. You are not a loser. None of us are.

Vince Lombardi once said, "I've never lost a game, I just ran out of time." I loved this when I first saw it. Why? Because that's a winning ATTITUDE.

Vince Lombardi knew that given the right conditions he could have turned it around. Given enough time, he could have made the right conditions appear. The same applies to you and me. In our careers and our professional world, given the right conditions and the right amount of time, we could make nearly anything happen in our favor.

What needs to go in your favor?

Are you a professional who seemed to always be in the right place at the right time in your career? Some of you may be saying, "Does that ever happen?" Yes, it does. If it hasn't happened to you, no worries, there's still time. <smiles> Are you the professional who for the first time is running into a snag? Job shift? Company acquisition? Layoff? The marketplace may seem a bit challenging, but it is worth it to stay confident. Even in the LOSS of what you've had, there's something new that's on its way.

Experiencing a LOSS can make you feel LOST. This is temporary. It's a transition. Some think, "Okay. Nice word. But really?" Yes. Really!

In 2007/2008, I was in transition having become a distressed business owner. I lost the fire to keep myself in the game. I decided to go back to work full-time for another company. A year and a half in, they laid me off. Thirty days later, my husband was laid off! Ouch! To top this off, my daughter's 16th birthday was approaching. She had been planning this for at least five years. I'm thinking Mickey D's. Okay! McDonald Land cookies all around. My daughter couldn't see the humor in that at all.

We were at a LOSS, but we were not losers. Failure is an EVENT, not a PERSON as Zig would say. Eventually, we landed on our feet! And the party events were a blast!!!

During these times of LOSS don't project meanings that are not real. Thoughts that you will never find another role. Thoughts that you did something wrong. Thoughts of WHY ME?

Now's the time to focus on who you ARE professionally and what VALUE you bring to the marketplace by identifying ALL of the things that make you the best at what you do. You have to rally around the positive. Positive activities. Positive people. Positive thoughts.

You know affirmations come to my mind. What one thing can you focus on that will keep you in the game even when you are not playing? Find one that suits your personality and hold on to it. Repeat daily. Put it on your mirror in the bathroom or even your refrigerator.

Pulling out of a loss may not be easy. If prolonged and unchecked, not only will you be in a loss place but even worse, the loss can be in you and that's why I must address this in the 26 Doses. I want you to get ahead of the thing and take it down.

Stay on the right side of a loss knowing that you are not the LOSS and that you are not the only one to have ever experienced a shift. Hold your head up and move on to the next DOSE.

✓ Check up

On a scale from 1 to 5, how do you feel when you recall your career losses? Lost? One being that you are not sure that you can overcome the hurdles of what should have been by now and maybe you have some resentments about what you have experienced and five being that when you revisit the past losses, if you ever do, you have handled the feeling pretty much and you've used the past to springboard into you now reality. _____

 Prescription

Read 7 Habits of Highly Effective People with a focus on Begin with the End in Mind. This chapter will help you get a sense reframing your experience. Next, in your workbook, write a list of five of your most memorable experiences as a professional. In the career management industry, there are several terms like "STAR" or "CAR" method. Write the experience to include what the problem was and what you contributed to it.

Additionally you could create a BRAG book, as a colleague of mine, Frank DeLaurentis, calls it. This book can be pages of, yes, things that are awesome about you! You can add, pictures, stories, letters of recommendation. It can contain things that ring YOUR bells about yourself professionally.

26 Doses of Career Triage

·

Show me a successful individual and I'll show you someone who had real positive influences in his or her life. I don't care what you do for a living—if you do it well I'm sure there was someone cheering you on or showing the way. A mentor." – Denzel Washington

Dose 13

Mentoring

Mentoring is a huge component of professional development. I believe it is a component that has strengthened so many people along their career path and has afforded them the ability to navigate changes like LOSS or lack of focus. People who have had the benefit of mentoring have attested to its usefulness and are GRATEFUL for those who have supported them in their journey.

In John Maxwell's Five Levels of Leadership, he refers to the "Level Four" Leader. This is a person who makes a point to develop others. I call it putting "self on a shelf". You have to be able to do this graciously so as to help another person in their endeavors. The level four leader is the person who becomes the eyes and ears of the less experienced professional by giving them the benefit of their own time-tested wisdom.

When I started my speaking career, I had several mentors from the National Speakers Association: Bill Thompson, Marjorie Brody, and Carol Kivler. Each had their own area of strength and were able to guide and support me in various ways. I gleaned from them invaluable information that helped me to navigate through what I had to do in order to become an influential and successful professional speaker. I approached them and requested their support and they were so gracious to accommodate me when their schedules permitted. In the world of Career Management insightful coaches such as Beth Wilson, Marlyn Kalitan and Lauri Plante "coached" me. Dr. Dennis Kimbro, a professor at Clark University in Atlanta, GA, who has written several Best Sellers and is a dynamic speaker has been influential in helping me to stay on the path of success.

All of these mentioned here were integral in my professional growth along with those with me in the professional trenches such as friend/mentor, Lemuel W. Woodson, whose business experience of over 35 years helped me to identify and engage new business endeavors. With his guidance and support my courage has increased and horizons have expanded.

As a professional, growth is always paramount. How can you grow? Of course, taking a class or reading a book comes to mind. But there are some things that books will not give you. You NEED a MENTOR. Mentors are a hand-up in the industry. A mentor is someone who can help you to avoid a pothole or two. I liken it to traveling. If you put your destination in, the GPS is going to give turn-by-turn guidance as you travel. Yet, if you, on your journey, come to a pothole in the street, the GPS, although adequate for travel, will not be able to see the pothole. But if there is someone in the car with you as a backseat driver, that person can say, "Hey, watch out for that pothole." That's the mentor. The GPS is akin to the book or online class. It provides as much as it can. But the mentor is more in the seat right next to you offering in-the-moment support.

Mentoring relationships vary though. I don't want to give the impression that you can or should call your mentor for EVERYTHING that occurs in your daily life. Not at all. However, as you are planning out and experiencing life, the mentor is that in-the-real-world guidance that can help at the moment and give personal/professional/perspective on your situation.

Having a mentor is important and I will stand by that statement. Also, being a mentor can be of great benefit to you as a professional.

We all have something to offer. You can mentor someone as far up the road as you have traveled yourself. I think about seeing a mother with several children. Maybe she's even pregnant with another one. There may be two children in a stroller, one child holding on to the stroller and an older child holding the hand of the younger child, each in step with the mom. The older one not pushing the stroller because that responsibility is for the adult, but the older child can hold the hand of the younger sibling, sharing what she/he can. That's how I see mentoring. Even if you don't have a Ph.D., you can teach an undergraduate class with your Master's. Find a "space" and what you have that makes a difference in the lives of other.

✓   Check up

Do you have any person or persons who you have engaged on a regular basis to be a sounding board or to act as an official mentor for you? Yes or No (Please circle one)

 Prescription

If yes, AWESOME. If no, you should add this into your professional world.

- Start by conducting a little more research on mentoring relationships
- Identify a viable mentor or two
- Move forward to forge a relationship

Also, consider becoming a mentor as well. There are many opportunities inside of corporations, with organizations like the Boys and Girls Clubs of America, inside of churches, and universities to name a few. Before engaging know what the time commitment is and ensure that it aligns with what you are able to fit into your life. When will you start? _____

26 Doses of Career Triage

If you want to go fast, go alone. If you want to go far, go with others. – African Proverb

Dose 14

Networking

Networking is about building relationships. It is said that your network work determines your net worth. But if the only thing you're trying to do is build your net worth, then networking in its truest sense is not going to facilitate that idea.

From the beginning of time, relationship building is a major step people take to get things done. Businesses such as Direct Sales or Networking Marketing have produced millionaires through providing business/services via their expanding networks of family and friends and then to the world. That cannot be disputed.

Why is networking important? Because it is! Ha!

Over the years, I have been blessed and fortunate enough to know and meet some awesome people with whom I have built great relationships. Some of these individuals, I met by way of networking. Networking can be a great tool when considering how to develop, strengthen and maintain your career.

Who do you know? Who do they know?

That's a great question.

My Godson, Derek, was about to graduate from High School. His mother, who is a long-time friend of mine happened to mention it to me saying that he was looking for a job at the time. I reached out to a friend who is a restaurant franchisee. He gave me the name of one of his colleagues in that same chain and I called. The owner was very kind. And said that he'd interview Derek that day. Because of that contact, Derek worked at the restaurant for five years.

You've leveraged your network before I am sure. Why is it that people get a little weary when it comes to doing the same thing for their careers/jobs? Some may feel that they don't know anybody, but sure you do. Check out one of the best memory joggers that I've seen in a while online at www.vivi-global.com. Get started thinking new and fresh.

A client of mine who is an attorney was laid off from his firm. Being a creature of habit, although he wasn't working, he still went to his dry cleaners every week but this time, not in a suit but in sweats. The dry cleaner noticed the change and my client explained that he had been laid off. The dry cleaner offered to introduce my client to another customer who came in every Thursday morning to drop off his suits/shirts for the week. My client showed up, dressed to the NINES. (Google it! <Smiles>). The Dry cleaner made the connection and several weeks later, my client was working again.

Who do you know?

If you are in the midst of a job search, I suggest that everyone you know become a part of your TEAM. Develop your DYNAMIC NETWORKING INTRO (In Presentation Chapter) and share it with everyone around you. After you've started, fine-tune it of course. This is TEAM YOU! You never know who that connector will be.

I learned that there are three types of networks:

- Personal – family, friends, acquaintances, colleagues.
- Operational – vendors and service providers.
- Strategic – mentors, coaches and some teachers.

Each of us have them. They can be powerful if understood and utilized appropriately. It is important to keep people in the appropriate "NETWORK" in which there are some expectations. For instance, you may need a person to do some updates on your website. You have a family member (personal network) who is a web developer as their trade, they could easily do the work for you and for FREE! Yippee! This will save you money. They say yes and you are happy. Time moves on. This family member may have a full-time job obligation and can only tend to your project on the weekends but this has to come secondary to their children's t-ball games on Saturdays and they don't want to work on Sundays at all. Weeks could possibly go by before any headway is made. That to say, even though the good intentions were there, it may serve you better to hire the right service provider (operational NETWORK), pay the MONEY and get the service you need to be done at the time you want the project to be completed. Now, your family member can still come to your house for Thanksgiving dinner. <smiles>

I have had raving experiences with people from my personal network and experiences that were great. Just so that you know! As President Obama would say, "Trust but verify"! <smiles>

Likewise, if you have a service provider that is not doing the job well, it's time to upgrade. You don't have a lot of time for slipshod work that doesn't serve the purpose and may have to be done repeatedly. It's a new day. You can choose those in operational and strategic networks to handle your projects.

One of my clients, Alex K. opened my eyes when he coined the phrase "NETWORK, or not work." I think this is powerful. Alex ran a classic textbook job campaign. He did all of the right things. What was amazing to me was the fact that his network was very responsive. Have you ever had to ask for recommendations or references? How long did that take? Unfortunately, it can be tragic if you are asked by a potential employer to give five references and the responses are needed in a week's time. In Alex's case, he had a response rate of several hours for about 10 references. That was simply amazing.

Our being able to contribute to our network proves our thoughtfulness and professionalism. We may not know how we are impacting someone's career when we don't get back to them.

Additionally, I believe that we should stay in touch with those in our network. Of course, LinkedIn can be helpful. I submit that there is nothing like a good old phone call or email and the age-old lunch. These can go a long way.

If we really want to blend the centuries, how about this…

I met a lady on LI named Betty. She and I had interacted on the platform for years. We'd "like" a post/comment and once in a while, she would send a message. Ultimately, we planned to meet at her church. We did so and it was so nice to put a face to a message. (Here's another "Don't try this at home boys and girls.")

But that to say that we must continue to build relationships that span pass our checkbooks and into our hearts.

Consider that your network really is only as strong as your contribution to it.

Lastly, it is important to build industry professional relationships that you can engage to help you grow and develop in the stage of your career where you are right now. What does that mean? Although there are thousands of online industry communities that you can join, I'd like you to consider joining at least one "brick and mortar" industry networking group. By that I mean a group that physically meets somewhere on a regular basis. This will build roots for you in your industry.

If you are going to outlast the changes in the marketplace, you have to possess these types of interrelations. This means joining a group or two. This can be time intensive and "people challenging" at times. This is where EMOTIONAL INTELLIGENCE comes into play. Because, as I know people to be, they *will* try you. That's just the bottom line. But I also believe that these experiences of getting to know people and engaging industry information firsthand can be invaluable.

✓ Check up

On a scale from 1 to 10 how do you score regarding staying connected with and or getting connected with people both personally and professionally? One being that you haven't been to any meetings/events in a LONG time and have not deliberately met anyone new in what seems to be eons to ten which means you are popping on all cylinders meeting and building relationships with people on a regular basis. _____

[Rx] Prescription

1. Let's start with considering your short-term goals for the next year. Consider what space that requires you to be in as far as your career is concerned. Are you going back to school? Are you looking for a new job? Create a list of five people that come to mind when you think

about this goal. Why did you think about them? Make time to reach out to them. "Hey, how are you? How has everything been? Listen, I am considering going back to school. As I was thinking about my plans you came to mind." This is an easy icebreaker. Take it from there.

2. Work on your LinkedIn profile. Don't have one? UGH!!!! Become more active on this platform. Look at what people are doing. Take an online course on how to use LinkedIn to build your network.

3. Become involved in your alumni associations. They would love to see you!

4. Join a brick and mortar association that is of interest to you.

Which will you do first? _____ When will you start?
_____

26 Doses of Career Triage

When we are no longer able to change a situation - we are challenged to change ourselves. — *Viktor Frankl*

Dose 15

Obstacles & Opportunities

If you have never had any obstacles, I am wondering right now, what are you doing. SMILES!

We all will have them. Obstacles come in all different shapes and sizes. I'm sure you've heard these words, "If what happens to you doesn't kill you, it will make you stronger." I am a witness to that.

Obstacles are a part of life and we should just settle in our minds that they will come our way. The question is dependent on how we handle them. Will we take them or will they take us? I will always go with the former. We must be prepared to overcome the obstacles that are headed our way. Recently I saw a post on LinkedIn that said, "So far, you've survived 100% of your worst days." The TRUTH!

We've discussed quite a few things that can prepare us for the

OBSTACLES that are ahead of us. To name a few:

- MENTORS
- ATTITUDE
- JOY
- BRAVERY
- COMMUNICATION
- DETERMINATION

As you go down this career path, you will encounter so many things. This is why this book is configured in this manner giving doses of encouragement to meet some of the situations you are faced with. Of course, there can be much more conversation around each of these subjects and in great depth. Yet, right now, we're hitting them in the center to expose either the benefit or detriment. Treatments are right around the corner.

What types of obstacles have you faced recently in your job? One of my clients recently experienced the rollout of a new payroll system. This did not take their company by surprise. BUT he was SURPRISED. Absolutely everything was in mild disarray. Each and every department in their company was impacted and this presented a huge obstacle. An OBSTACLE to employees getting paid the correct amount and the amounts being accounted for properly and so on. He had an OBSTACLE to his own peace of mind. Yet, this obstacle was upon him. What should he do? Even though he is not in a strategic leadership role regarding this rollout, his involvement was still important. My suggestion to him was that he become a solution to this new OBSTACLE we started calling an OPPORTUNITY. He had to set out to learn more about the inner workings of this system that apparently the vendor has not prepared them to know or understand. In doing so, he would be able to provide much needed support for everyone around him. His taking the OBSTACLE and converting it into an Opportunity has now positioned him for more responsibility and respect. Who knows? Maybe a promotion, bonus or raise. Regardless of how it ultimately rolls out, he will be able to relieve himself of the headaches that always accompany an OBSTACLE because he will now have the answer.

I recently heard a story about a farmer whose donkey fell into a ditch. The ditch was so deep that it was going to be impossible for them to heave the donkey out. They were convinced that the only thing that they could do was to "put the donkey out of its misery". The farmer took a shovel and started to toss dirt into the hole. [All of my animal lovers, hold on, it gets better]. The donkey was crying out and shuffling its hooves as the dirt was being slowly tossed into the hole. What ended up happening was the donkey was stepping on it and packing the dirt down. This began to fill the hole until the dirt was high enough for the donkey to be lifted out of the hole. AMAZING! Happy ending!

We all will face OBSTACLES, but how we approach them can determine whether they bury us or lift us to a new level of success.

Your career depends on your ability to overcome the OBSTACLES ahead of you with skill and ease. You will show yourself as one that has what it takes to not only survive but thrive. It will also showcase that if you are not in a leadership role, you probably can attain one. AND if you are in leadership, you are the right person. OBSTACLES are what we can use to exercise our problem-solving muscles. Sometimes, the muscles are needed to move the OBSTACLE. Sometimes the brain muscle is needed to hold off on immediate action, so the problem will work itself out. How to come to this knowledge requires wisdom which comes free but it's not cheap.

✓   Check up

Do you have any goals that are being held up?   Yes or No?

_____

What is the goal?

_____

_____

_____

What appears to be the hold up?

_____

_____

R̶x̶ Prescription

Write in your book the answers to these two questions. Then "reverse engineer" your solution which may include a mild session of root cause analysis. You can find the details on how that can be done online. Look at your "obstacle", determine what you CAN do, do that, revisit your progress and repeat. Do this until you break through to the other side toward your goal.

For example if you are an IT professional, you might want to increase your salary to live more comfortably but your company has a "freeze" on salaries at this time. If you don't mind moving to another company, that might be your answer. But if you really want to stay where you are, and you are not open to working a second job or starting a business consider what you CAN CONTROL in this situation. If you cannot control the INCOME at this point you can surely control the OUTGO which will effectively increase the money you have available to you. This could give you the OPPORTUNITY to be creative and find new things that you may have not thought of before.

Let's OVERCOME the OBSTACLES! Seize the OPPORTUNITIES!

If you're presenting yourself with confidence, you can pull off pretty much anything. – Katy Perry

Dose 16

Presentation

How we show up as professionals can be critical to our ability to influence others and to establish our mark in our career or our jobs. The topic of PRESENTATION holds a near and dear space in my heart because I am a communicator both in front of the room and beyond.

I started the journey as a Toastmaster at Raytheon Engineers Toastmasters in Philadelphia, PA. There, I suffered much at the hands of great evaluators like Miki Baker and Ryan Nemeroff and my MENTOR, Priscilla Gabosch. I worked long and hard to develop the skills they were telling me I should have like not dropping the "g" off of the end of a word, and the infamous "put the pocket flap inside on both sides of your jacket". Yes. That does make a difference when being observed by an audience. You can see that I am still scarred by it. <smiles>

How you show up is important. In your career, you may never have had to stand in front of the room and deliver a speech or present an idea. What if you got the opportunity today? Would you be ready? That's the question. When is the time to be ready? Yesterday!

So get on it.

Everyone shows up differently on the stage. I don't suggest that you show up like Les Brown. Although if you do, please send me a VIP ticket. However, I am suggesting that you should be as prepared as you can be and be able to make a whole lot of sense, so much so that when you sit down, you say, "YES!" to yourself. You would want to know that you can do it well if eventually asked.

That said, this dose of Career Triage is to encourage you to get your speak on. Become a capable deliverer of a message from the stage, in a small group or one-on-one.

Another piece of your ability to present is to be able to present yourself to another person in a short understandable statement that many call the elevator speech or 30-Commercial. I have dubbed it the Dynamic Networking Intro which you can find in the back of this book. Regardless of what you call it, I believe that we all should have one. Some would say, "I know how to introduce myself." Possibly, but, will it be clear and effective? A real Dynamic Networking Intro leaves your hearer with a clear sense of who you are professionally. Yes, this can be done in 30-45 seconds. It is an art AND a science. The science is learning a structure. The art is delivering it with great confidence and ease. You can do this. Simply follow the structure of the Intro. What you want to communicate is who you really are, what you have done and what you can do! If you are in a NETWORKING situation while in transition, you can say what you are looking to find as far as work is concerned. Be flexible with this and show the world who you are.

The last aspect of PRESENTATION I would want to cover here while I have your attention is your wardrobe. Yes, what you wear. In some work environments, casual dress is okay. By and large, it is acceptable and everybody's doing IT. But therein is the problem, EVERYBODY is doing it. I want you to stand out. Yes! Like a good sore thumb because you don't want to be like everybody. It will be okay. Trust me.

I started my professional career in a work environment that was business formal. Nearly everyone wore professional clothes. Suits and ties were the norm. And yes, nice pantsuits and dresses for the women. I know that was more than twenty years ago, yet I will say that the people who will dwarf the competition are those who STILL dress for where they are going. I had this conversation with a client the other day. Yes, take the hit and buy several new vital pieces for your wardrobe! I don't believe that she has to be super formal every day BUT she may be called to an unexpected meeting. That meeting could very well include the PROVOST of her institution. Not probable but POSSIBLE. I suggested that she always have a NICE black jacket that she can put on, on her way to that unexpected meeting. The jacket will certainly pull stuff together immediately. TaDa! She would now look the part. Regardless of what anyone will tell you, how you look does influence what they think about you. Use this knowledge to your advantage.

For the younger professional, if you want to be taken seriously, start by improving how you look. Hair or lack thereof and your wardrobe. I guarantee it will set you above the rest.

Another client I worked with wanted to change the perception of his superiors towards him and the wardrobe was all he changed. Amazingly, he was taken more seriously and was included in more important meetings. Promoted. What you wear is not the "begin all end all" but it does make a statement. IJS (which means "I'm just sayin'")!

———————————

✓ Check up

Ask a trusted astute forward moving colleague or mentor to give you an evaluation on how you "show". Ask the about things like:

- Actual presentation skills
- Attire and overall "look"
- Impact as a professional / influence

Listen to what they have to say.

℞ Prescription

Take note of what your conversation(s) with your colleague yielded. If there are areas where they have indicated that you could be better, get to it. Additionally do some research on Executive Presence. There is a lot of material available on it. Also consider joining Toastmasters International if you need help with presentation skills. There's a club near you: www.toastmasters.org.

26 Doses of Career Triage

Quality means doing it right when no one is looking –
Henry Ford

Dose 17

Quality/Quantity

Dose 17! These both matter. I have learned that there are only two ways to do something... Right. Or... AGAIN. Believe it.

As your career is unfolding, look back on how you deliver what you deliver. Are you a person who delivers a HIGH-QUALITY product or service? Can your leader walk away knowing that not only will you get it done but that it will be done well?

Unfortunately, I don't know that our society expects good quality anymore. How many times have you left the drive-thru of your favorite fast-food establishment, make it home and found that something was missing OR wrong? Yes, you ordered the triple burger but you said NO CHEESE! And not only was there cheese, but there were two slices instead of the normal one. Now, I don't leave the window or the store without checking every single thing down to tasting the beverage.

QUALITY should not be a thing of the past especially with so many options out there. But then, which OPTION will give you less wrong becomes the prevailing question.

Are YOU producing a QUALITY service or product? Do you

go above and beyond to ensure that what leaves your hands is what they expect or more? Or have you been lulled into what people will accept? Which means how you can just get by, by being marginal. And not EXCELLENT. Take pride in yourself and what has your name on it.

We always want to put our best foot? forward because it represents who we truly are. If our QUALITY leads the way, then our career can surely follow suit.

It can be difficult to be a person who produces a QUALITY product. What does that even look like? Has anyone ever told us? Does anybody even know or care?

In some industries, exactness is very important such as accounting, manufacturing, and science. There are many industries where QUALITY is in the eye of the beholder. When we think of stores, which one comes to mind when we think of the highest quality? Nordstrom? When we think of cars, which one do we expect to be top-notch in every category? Bentley? Of course, these are the exceptional examples, I admit. But to this point, why can't we be that exceptional example as well. We should be.

In addition to QUALITY, we should be able to "kick it up a notch" ala Emeril Lagasse and put out the requisite QUANTITY of that product or service. If not. Why not?

I used to work as a claims examiner for a life insurance company. Yes, I have had quite a few jobs in my day. <smiles> At my level, I was expected to produce 26 (funny number uh?) claims a day. And that was it. Anything less was regarded as unproductive and they would look at you sideways. Anything more was ignored; just 26. This is true confessions... I did 27 claims/day every day with about three hours to spare. Could I have done more? Absolutely. Was I inclined to do more? Absolutely not. Why? Number one; I did not know then what I know now and Number two, anything beyond 26 was totally ignored. On both ends, if we had known better we could have done better. In my producing these claims, I proved that I deserved my job. They were done right! But I did not employ some of the things I'm sharing with you now. I mean, the things I have learned in my many years in the workforce and my over 20 years as a career coach.

Once you are a person that can produce a QUALITY move into upping your game by producing more than is expected of you, or if you can do both, you are definitely setting yourself up for the next level. This may come by way of promotion or you will have the time to promote yourself out of the door. EXIT stage left. Either way, the QUANTITY will not hurt you.

✓ Check up

On a scale of 1 to 5 how do you see the work product and service that you deliver personally? One being that you are often requested to redo or follow up on what you have produced, you receive poor ratings or notice that you are hardly ever lauded by customers/clients/superiors/coworkers for a job well-done. Five meaning that you are often thanked for your efforts, specifically requested for service or projects and/or are requested by my leaders to train others on various tasks. _____

R̽ Prescription

To raise your level of quality, you must raise your own standards. If you know that you have not been producing at a high level of quality and you are STILL employed, GRATITUDE ought to kick in right now! Moving forward you must change this. This aspect of your career will catapult you to the next level. Do these things:

Become a student of your work. Learn everything that pertains to what you do which includes the specific tasks and exactly HOW they should be done; know and understand the workflow around your specific tasks/job efforts (i.e. if you are an administrative assistant get to know what ALL of the other departments/divisions do and the main people in each department); and read information on your company and embrace the vision and culture of the company.

Take PRIDE in everything you do. Ask yourself if you'd wear it or buy or come back for more of whatever it is that you produce.

Reread the FOCUS DOSE and use that prescription as well.

Begin to produce more. If you have a quota, once you have improved your quality, exceed your quota. If you don't have a quota, seek ways to produce more and add more VALUE to your team.

Create a simple plan here:

I will

_____

By _____

In order to

_____

26 Doses of Career Triage

Change before you have to. – Jack Welch

Dose 18

Relevance

As a professional, you may have noticed that the world is always changing. Hey! Even as I am writing this, I am certain that something has changed. There is no question. As a professional, we must always stay relevant.

The funniest thing… As I was writing this book and gathering quotes, I had a difficult time finding a relevant quote for this dose. The irony! But I was DETERMINED to make it happen.

Pull off these doses together, my friend. It is about relevance. We have to find our space in the marketplace. Yes. Yet, in doing so, remember that everything is always moving at a fast pace. So we must be and stay relevant.

Several years ago, you may recall that Microsoft decided that they were no longer going to support Windows 7. As I chugged along with my laptop which had that operating system, I ignored the impending doom of the change. My laptop was getting slower and slower. I continued to hear that the changeover was coming. Obviously, this was going to be a BIG thing but I still did not make the requisite move. I kept on using my laptop with Windows 7 on it. Not only was the operating system old but the release on Outlook was doomed to fail as well. At that point, there were no system updates and I was on my own with this thing. Logging on was a day-by-day experience. The bell was tolling for me!

Finally, one day, I came to my senses and I decided to buy a new laptop. I got on the phone and ordered it. This was a Monday at about 10:00 AM EST. I hung up the phone. Whew! Alright, I ordered it. Now, I'm cool. I turned my laptop on and it totally locked up. FEAR struck my heart. OMG! The screen went dark, immediately panic set in. If there would have been music playing, it would have been the theme from the TWILIGHT ZONE.

I jumped up from my couch thinking that I could go to BEST BUY. Maybe they could bypass the login to boot up the system so I could get back in until my new laptop arrived in two days. I was crazy! I went to BEST BUY and they gave me the worst news ever. "Sorry, ma'am, we cannot bypass the login. Our contract with Microsoft prohibits us from doing anything with Windows 7. We are bound by the agreement."

Are you kidding me!?!?!?!?

What was I going to do? I had data in the computer that had not been backed up. I stood in shock trying to think but my brain was literally frozen in time.

Can you hear the Jeopardy music right now?

I asked them if they could retrieve the data from my hard drive? The answer was yes. This would cost me several hundreds of dollars and a duration of two days.

Basically, there was no one who couldn't convinced me that my laptop knew it was getting ready to be out and decided to make the move first! I am not kidding or smiling right now. Relevance!

I was so outdated that I could not be helped even by the GEEK SQUAD!

Don't let that be your case for you can do better. Stay on top of what is happening in the marketplace. EDUCATION, VALUE, YOUTHFULNESS/YEARS and WORTH. All important to your RELEVANCE. I can't say it any more clearly than that.

I am usually heartbroken when I talk to someone that has worked for many years at a company or in a particular role. With little to no RELEVANT skills under their belt, they find themselves in the marketplace needing a job. This is truly a hard thing to face.

No one wants to say it, but I must write it here. My friends, do not be in a career by default. Take full charge of who you are professionally and where you are going. It is a must. Keep your eyes and ears open to what's happening. And like with Windows 7, when the handwriting is more than on the WALLS, you shouldn't be found running to BEST BUY's of career management needing a fix that is not going to happen. Or at least not as soon as you may need it.

BE RELEVANT and STAY RELEVANT.

It is a daunting task because it does mean that you will have to put time and effort and maybe money into your career. If you have not done this in a while, then get started. Your effort here will pay off in the long run.

Again, "By any means necessary."

One caution, here… Even if you are in a field that is going well, anything less than an "A" deserves your attention. How can you get the most out of your day taking into consideration HEALTH, FOCUS, DETERMINATION, SUCCESS, QUALITY/QUANTITY and VALUE? Did I forget anything?

When time is gone, it is indeed gone. It can never be recaptured. I know we have all had those feelings of having lost out on this or that because we did not utilize our time appropriately or effectively. Being diligent here to assign our time appropriately. Visit and/or revisit the prescriptions for the DOSES that I have mentioned above.

Is it time to regroup? If so, how will you realign yourself to get the most out of your day. Do these:

- Identify the priorities of the day, the night before is best as in the FOCUS DOSE
- Be aware to not be too optimistic by scheduling way too many things to get done in a day. That's a setup for continued failure
- Apply the 4 D's of Time Rescue as outlined in Dose 20 (Do this as often as necessary). This will harness unruly demands on your time.
- Add breaks into your schedule purposefully
- Celebrate your accomplishments

The tides may shift. If we are on the wrong side of the shift, it may be a bumpy road for us. Stay attuned to what you need to do. This will help you to stay afloat as tides change. You will be able to get your bearings straight in order to make a proper switch.

In the EDUCATION dose, I made mention of Beth who was

able to make adjustments in her career that landed her safely as things changed in her company. There are other stories from that same situation that did not go well as planned. Some of the other IT professionals in her department who did not avail themselves to training beyond their current "job description," were faced with the same issue. The newer technologies that were introduced into their company did not require support for the old systems. Those who did not even know the name of the newer technologies found themselves with severance packages and leaving a very nice company where they had been for over 20 years. Their skills were useful in the marketplace but not at a salary that they were used to. Being priced out of the market is called GOLDEN HANDCUFFS. I don't know how or when these folks landed, but I am sure they did. Yet, I do know that it would have been much easier on them if they were prepared and had RELEVANT skills for the new direction the company was taking.

It is not easy to stay in tuned to what's going on. After all, we're all working. However, it is a must for us to carve out time to delve into what is happening around us. I can attest to this myself. Even though I may know what is happening in the marketplace with this new development or the latest and greatest book on the shelves, sometimes I lack in the area of the world news. A friend of mine ALWAYS says, "Janice, you need to know what's going on in the world." Honestly, I try to get it in; some days I do and some days I don't. That's why I need friends. <smiles> Easy for me say but I admit this because I want you to know that I know it's not going to be easy. You must do it though. Your profession depends on it.

———————————

✓ Check up

Do you feel that you could comfortably talk with another person in your same field about today's marketplace regarding what you do? Yes being that you can hold your own and offer responses as well as thoughts/ideas about where your industry is and is going in the future. No meaning that you really are not aware enough about technologies, new skills, current marketplace demand or where your current employer is in the scheme of things. _____

R̲x̲ Prescription

I believe we all need a CHECK UP FROM THE NEXT UP here! Being relevant is one thing STAYING relevant is GOLDEN.

Here are a few things to do to brush up quickly:

Find out what "industry" segment your current company is considered to be in. List it here:

_____

List three of your employer's industry competitors:

_____

_____

_____

Visit your company's website and review its pages and become acquainted with what the world sees about what you do. Register to receive a monthly newsletter if they have one.

Consider the occupation/career that you are in (i.e. Accounting, Customer Service, Information Technology and so on). Conduct some research about your individual professional industry on the Bureau of Labor and Statistics website at www.bls.gov . You could start with the "Career" segment in the upper right hand on the toolbar. Pick a category that interests you and follow it through. This is about familiarity right now not mastery.

Stay determined to keep abreast of what is happening and move accordingly.

Success is doing what you have been designed to do and doing it well. – Janice Coleman

Dose 19

Success

How do you define success?

_____

_____

_____

_____

_____

I believe there are many factors we can look at, but the only true gauge of success is the intent of purpose. What do I mean by that? Let me tell you the story of the doorstop.

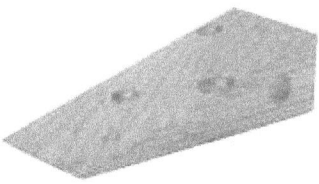

Everyone at some time or another has seen a doorstop, right? It's a pretty common looking thing. Its sole intent and purpose is to keep a door open. There are not too many sizes of doorstops, maybe several colors and maybe different material like rubber and wood. Again the sole purpose of a doorstop is to keep a door open. As I consider it, it is a pretty small thing to accomplish the job it performs. It is uniquely designed for that purpose.

Question…

What else can you think of that can be used to keep a door open? Make a list here:

_____

_____

_____

_____

_____

Let me just offer some ideas to go with the ones you already have here: A rope, a person, a trash can, a chair, a folded-up piece of paper and a cinder block. Did we miss anything?

All of these things have been used at some time or another to keep a door open. Yet, there is not one of them that does it as SUCCESSFULLY as a doorstop. You may say "Oh, yes, they do it fairly well, Janice." To that, I would agree BUT the success the doorstop has that nothing else on our lists can claim is the fact that it was performing the task for which it was actually designed. It's small enough to keep the door open without any hassle, maneuvering, continual fixing into place, taking up too much space and so on.

The rope is used for jumping. The trashcan is for trash. The chair is used for us to sit on. The folded-up piece of paper should be unfolded and written upon, and the cinder block is useful for building. A person is useful in managing all of the other things listed here. The doorstop is the ONLY thing on this list of items that when used to keep a door open is uncategorically SUCCESSFUL.

SUCCESS is doing what you have been designed to do and doing it well. Anything else other than this entails abnormal use, which is ABUSE.

Our goal in life, as we navigate the world and find our work in it, is to find the work for which we really have been designed to do AND do THAT!

It is only when you are doing what you are good at that you will find the true meaning of SUCCESS. Of course, we may have accomplishments along the way in our lives. However, when we hit true success, days will be happier and our sleep will be sweeter. I know my SUCCESS is found in my ability to help people to Live Out Loud, Play Full Out AND Be Invincible in Their SPACE. I do that by exercising the innate giftings that I have along with the knowledge that I have gained ON my path. How I brought forth that gift is through speaking, coaching, training, teaching, mentoring and now writing.

There are so many outlets that we have through which we can experience life's successes. They will all be wrapped up into who we are becoming. Do you know people who have found SUCCESS in one area of their life but are still coming along in another area? Of course, I will raise my hand to that. But we must keep on moving. It is only by DETERMINATION that we will find our SUCCESSES. When we do find them, we must acknowledge them. Yes! Do not hold back on patting yourself on the back regarding the things in which you are SUCCESSFUL. This will help you to be mindful of your WORTH and VALUE. It will bring JOY and fuel your ZEAL during your challenging times.

Your SUCCESS will keep you mindful that you are able to do anything worthwhile and that is what you are supposed to do.

I used to have a magnet on my refrigerator that says, "SUCCESS COMES in CANS, not CAN'Ts."

Finding true purpose in your life helps to support your career path and maybe even give a little course correction from time to time.

The gentleman that I mentioned in the article in the dose on VALUE is a prime example. He had a love for graphic design and had started out his career doing that. He did not finish a degree in it but did have some notable SUCCESSES along his journey. Through the happenings of life, he found himself working at the department store where I met him. We had several conversations regarding what he would do if he could do anything in his life at that point in time. His heart was to be back in the real design world. Little did I know he was around 50 years old at that time. His YOUTHFULNESS did not peek through his YEARS to me, and we parted ways. Months later, I reached out to him by phone only to find out that he had decided to go back to school for a degree at a notable art school. He was in the midst of his program. It was very challenging and fulfilling to him. He is now working on projects that are bringing him back into the throws of the design world and he will be graduating in a year's time. He is feeling the freedom of following his passion and the whiff of the SUCCESS that is on the way. Was he accomplished while working in the store? Yes because he helped me. Others as well, I'm sure. But the SUCCESS that is coming dwarfs what he may have felt while helping people like me. I applaud him for charting a new path for himself that will be a SUCCESS based on what he feels inclined to do.

✓ Check up

On a scale of 1 to 10, how happy are you with what you are producing in your life? One being that you do not have a level of self-satisfaction, feeling that you are not contributing near the level you desire nor do you feel that what you do represents your best. Ten being that you are on it on a regular basis and you know that what you are contributing to this world is making the difference that you are happy with and of which you are proud.

⎯

℞ Prescription

You have been designed for a reason. Ask yourself several questions:

What is it that I do that makes me happy as I serve/help others:

• _____

- _____

- _____

- _____

What is it that people always ask of me in service or product:

- _____

- _____

- _____

- _____

What are you good at doing?

- _____

- _____

Ask a close professional colleague the same questions. Somewhere in these responses you will find a sweet spot to focus on. Out of that sweet spot will come a purpose. Work on that purpose, applying what you've learned in this book. You will find SUCCESS. Do not hold your feet to the fire forever on what you provide to the world because OPPORTUNITIES will come and may lead you into new areas where you will become more of what you are. Congratulate yourself in your accomplishments and continue to conquer new things with excellence.

God's Minute: I've only just a minute,
Only sixty seconds in it.
Forced upon me, can't refuse it,
Didn't seek it, didn't choose it,
But it's up to me to use it.
I must suffer if I lose it,
Give an account if I abuse it,
Just a tiny little minute,
But eternity is in it. – Dr. Benjamin E. Mays

Dose 20

Time

What can I say about time? We only have 168 hours in a week. That's it. That's sobering. I wish there was the ability for us to petition for more. But based on what I know about time and eternity, we are not getting more time added to our clocks. We are regulated to ENOUGH TIME.

Both the genius and the unlearned have the same amount of time. Both the rich and the poor. Both the quick and the slow. Both the competent and the incompetent. Both the meticulous and the careless. Both the wise and the foolish. Both Michael Jordan and the 50-year-old brother hangin' out on the school yard courts at night. We all have been given the same amount of time.

Since we know that time is fixed as noted in the Time Management MATRIX that Covey shares, we must agree that there is something that goes into every equation where time is involved to render the outcomes that the world sees from us. I believe that element is the PURPOSEFULNESS with which we use the time that we have.

All things being equal here, I am going to be referring to those of us who generally have the faculties to be level headed and are reasonably okay with mixing it up in the world. People like you, my friend. Yes. People who would be inclined to read a book like this or others in this genre of professional development. I am gearing all of these comments to people who want SUCCESS and maybe those of us who by definition are SUCCESSFUL.

Why talk about time? Because it is important. It is a resource that we ALL have and in the same quantity. It's a level playing field right here. Time. A real equalizer. Eyeball to eyeball, we are all the same.

Why is it then that there are the rich and the poor? Why are there the accomplished and the unfulfilled? Why are there the educated and the uneducated?

It comes down to how it is that we use the time that we are given. There are many ways to slice and dice it, yet it will soon come down to this in our equation. Because we can all start at 9:00 AM and end at 5:00 PM for five days a week. But when the paychecks are deposited, one person receives $360.00 and another receives $2,000.00. What's that all about?

There is a lot more that goes in, not just the equation. EDUCATION, PRESENTATION, ATTITUDE, EMOTIONAL INTELLIGENCE, NETWORKING, VALUE, WORTH......

You know what I mean.

We can use the time we have to FOCUS our efforts toward the improvement on any and ALL of these factors right here and even more. We can also learn how to leverage our time with practices like my Four D's of Time Rescue. This is based on a quadrant formula, just like many developmental tools use for their presentation. If you are crammed for time, you simply never have enough. Get rescued by implementing this:

- **DO it!** Simply schedule the thing you need or want to do. Put your mind to it and FOCUS and DO it!
- **DELAY it!** Sometimes, things roll around on our schedule for days or weeks and we keep putting them off. In your head you want to do it but it's not a priority. Delay it! Officially take it off of your schedule and add it to another day. A week down the line or even a month or two. Put it on the schedule to do it. What does this do for you? Psychologically, it frees you from the disappointment of not accomplishing it and you now have given yourself a new start. Don't even think about it until the rescheduled date comes up and then DO it!
- **DELEGATE it!** You can start by handing off some things to someone else either at work or at home. When you delegate, ensure that you are clear about what needs to be done. There are several reasons to decide who you should delegate to; a person who needs to learn something new; a person who is expert and already capable; or a person who needs more work. Either way, the process should be to ALWAYS communicate exactly what needs to be done; 1) Show them; 2) Do it with them; 3) Watch them; and 4) Inspect it after the fact. Ultimately get it off your plate.
- **DITCH it!** Ask yourself if this really needs to be done or if it is a nice thing to do. If it does not need to be done, then DITCH it! Get it out of your life. Don't go through it anymore. Clear your desk. Clear your life! Move on.

Now, you will have the time you need to be SUCCESSFUL.

Sometimes, we will all fall into the time trap. Our careers can suffer because we don't make good use of time effectively either at work, preparing for work or building a new skill to be more apt for the tasks at hand. Use the minutes we have every day. They do add up.

✓ Check up

When you consider how you utilize time, how do you grade yourself A through F? _____

R Prescription

Anything less than an "A" deserves your attention. How can you get the most out of your day taking into consideration HEALTH, FOCUS, DETERMINATION, SUCCESS, QUALITY/QUANTITY and VALUE? Did I forget anything?

When TIME is gone, it is indeed gone. It can never be recaptured. I know we have all had those feelings of having lost out on this or that we did not utilize our TIME appropriately or effectively. Be diligent here to assign your TIME appropriately. Visit and/or revisit the prescriptions for the DOSES that I have mentioned above.

Is it time to regroup? If so, how will you realign yourself to get the most out of your day. Do these:

- Identify the priorities of the day, the night before is best as in the FOCUS DOSE.

- Be aware to not be too optimistic by scheduling way too many things to get done in a day. That's a setup for continued failure.
- Apply the 4 D's of Time Rescue that's outlined in this DOSE (Do this as often as necessary).
- Add breaks into your schedule purposefully.
- Celebrate your accomplishments.

Be YOU! There is no competition. — Unknown

Dose 21

Uniqueness

In the catalog of people on the planet of who has ever been here and those yet to come, YOU are the only YOU. You are UNIQUE. You were made with kid gloves. So important are you that you have 10 to 20 billion miles of DNA in your body and that DNA is specific only to you. That is powerful.

When you were conceived, there were over 20 million sperm released and ONLY one made it to the one egg in your mother's uterus which multiplied into who we know you now to be. Even if you are an IDENTICAL twin, your fingerprints and your DNA are still different.

You can't be any more UNIQUE than that. Yet, our world is hell-bent on stressing us out because we don't conform to its standards. It is our nature to be UNIFORM and not to CONFORM.

Conformity coincides with comparison. This is one of the reasons we experience SELF-WORTH issues.

I am not tall enough or short enough

I am not black enough or white enough

I am not smart as this Bill Gates

I am not likable as the most popular "girl" in school

I don't have as much money as Warren Buffet

I don't live in the right neighborhood

I didn't attend the right university

I am not as funny as Kevin Hart

I am not as loveable as Mother Teresa

On and on and on…

It will be never-ending UNTIL we stop it. Because enough is not enough.

We do not have to and should not desire to conform to anything other than the person we are becoming; the one you have in your heart and the SUCCESSFUL person you are working on PRESENTING to the world. Yes, that's the one we are to conform to. That is the fullness of our UNIQUENESS.

I had a challenging time with my UNIQUENESS. If you know me, you will know that I am pretty hard to miss being 6' tall. I never liked to leave late or leave early because I would not be missed. It was my UNIQUENESS, not in height, but goals, talents, and dreams, that I believe made me feel uncertain in groups with people who all seem to be in the same space. Or at least they were willing to portray that to the world. They never rocked the boat. Me? I always seemed to rock the boat. Asking the question OR having the answer.

Once a friend, Denise, told me not to worry. I would always be on the outside. She listed a few things that made me different like tall, slender, articulate, stylish, intelligent, determined and more. For caution of going too far, I'll stop there! <smiles> I am UNIQUE! NOW at 58, I can honestly say that it is this UNIQUENESS that makes me SUCCESSFUL. This is because it is me.

Your UNIQUENESS is what is going to make you even more SUCCESSFUL. Learn to LEAN into it. What do I mean?

> ➤ If you love to cook, why not take some classes that will teach you a new element of culinary arts that you were not aware of.
> ➤ If you really look good in BLUE, make that your signature color. Which may be different than your favorite color.
> ➤ If you have a nice voice, take a course on voiceovers.
> ➤ If you have a nicely decorated home, become the go-to person for young people furnishing their new living spaces.
> ➤ If you are smart, unashamedly use it to your advantage. Not as a "KNOW-IT-ALL" but as a helpful resource to others.
> ➤ If you are funny, try your hand at stand-up comedy. If you get big, don't forget to send me some tickets. <smiles>

Learn to love the things about yourself that make you UNIQUE. Embrace them and work to enhance them.

One client told me that her UNIQUENESS was that she says what's on her mind. We worked with that for a minute. Not that it was not a UNIQUE trait that she knew she possessed, but for her way of delivery, which made me pause. I asked her how we could COMMUNICATE that in a way that would be more intriguing….. We thought and she came back with. "I am able to share my perspective with others in a way that helps them to see the risk and reward of what they intend to do." Wordy? Maybe. Which do you like better? Really... Which is more UNIQUE? In an interview, I'm likin' that you can share your perspective. Frankly, most places have way too many people saying what's on their minds!

In an earlier dose, I mentioned my program ARE YOU HYPED. In that program, I talk about something called the HYPE HANDLE. This is an aspect of who you are that is your UNIQUENESS. One of my close friends, is a prolific relationship builder. His HYPE HANDLE is the Connector. This is not something he tries to do. It comes naturally and he just does it. He is wired that way. All of his personality is well-suited for that very thing. On top of all of the other skills he has, this is another aspect of his UNIQUENESS.

Some potential HYPE HANDLES are: BUILDER, MOTIVATOR, CREATOR, MATCH-MAKER, CONNECTOR, MR. or MRS. MAGIC, POWERHOUSE and so forth. If one of these fits, you can carry it as yours. If nothing there suits your fancy, then you should know that this is about UNIQUENESS, and so you should create the one that represents a solid facet of YOU.

My HYPE HANDLE is the Reign Maker because I prepare people to perform, along with the other aspects of how I support individuals in their growth and development.

We are more than likely in an industry that has other professionals that do what we do, yet, there should still be a UNIQUENESS about us. That is the things we can stand flatfooted and attest to as our strength and VALUE. As you build and fortify your career, being UNIQUE will serve you and will also help stand out in a crowd. Find yours and work it to your advantage and for the benefit of those who support and serve.

✓ Check up

What is one thing about yourself that you feel makes you stand out? _____

Do you see it as a "good" thing? Why or why not?

_____

_____

_____

R̽ Prescription

Consider that thing and how you could build or develop that skill/talent/characteristic/ability so that it can become a part of what you are known for. Very much like your BRAND. For example, Gregory Porter is a popular Jazz Vocalist. He has a great sound. But what makes him most UNIQUE is the shawl-like wrap that he wears under his hat. Um... Who knows why? Style? Cover up? Regardless, it is the most UNIQUE thing about him. He has embraced it and it is a part of who he is to the public.

How can this UNIQUENESS become a self-accepted part of what makes you UNIQUE as you bring YOU to the world?

_____

_____

My goal has always been to add value, not to be redundant, not to get in the way, but to do things that lift and move things forward in a very strategic and objective way so that there are real outcomes. – Michelle Obama

Dose 22

Value

When I think about bringing VALUE to any professional situation, I always start with the following concept I outline in my article, Be the one in your industry– The Tiered Career Strategy©. I have included it here:

"One very important part of improving your positioning in your industry is to become an expert in your field. Of course, you might say that is pretty sophomoric, Janice. But I say maybe not. Here's why…

Early on in my professional life, I was in the Information Technology industry and worked primarily in the Insurance sector. My last full-time IT work experience was with a leader in the Health Care industry. I had the privilege of working with some great professionals. During that time, the director of my department deposited something into me professionally that I will never forget.

She was an awesome leader and a great business partner in the financial segment of the company which consisted of every department that reported to the CFO. She had the ear of everyone, not just because she had the position but because they trusted her as a leader of the company. In John Maxwell's Five Levels of Leadership, I would rank her at four. She was a person who didn't mind sharing her knowledge because someone did it for her. She was bright, energetic and a people developer. She was awesome in my perspective and I respected her as did everyone who knew her.

One day, she and I had a "sit down" to discuss my career path at the company and she told me how to become invaluable. We both understood that at that time most people considered IT as an expense center and terribly difficult to understand. We were known for talking "computerese" and everyone dreaded status meetings. As we talked, this maverick explained how I could possibly leverage my career:

BECOME AN EXPERT IN YOUR FIELD

Regardless of your field of endeavor, you MUST become a student of that field and be the BEST! Be a ravenous learner. If this is not your NORM, start off slowly. Pick one media outlet, gradually follow it and grow. I found a new APP, *FLIPBOARD*. It has great information about almost anything you can think of. Get started! Be the one!!!

BECOME YOUR CUSTOMER

We must get into the customers' heads and know what they know and even more about *their* world. My director explained to me that, at that time, she belonged to several insurance associations and that she received their magazines. She was equipped to provide support to her business partners. She was an IT professional inside a health care company supporting financial professionals. She *tiered* her career and it worked for her. And it will for you too! Be the one!!!

BECOME THE ONE

Recently, I was in preparation for a GALA fundraiser for an

organization I support. I decided to take particular care with my entire "look". ON PURPOSE. I set out to find the *RIGHT* everything since and I believe I was successful. I ended up at a well-known department store for shoes. I met a gentleman there who was extraordinary. He seemed mild-mannered and eager to help me. I picked a few pairs of shoes and requested my size. He, another salesperson and I engaged in conversation. In the blink of an eye, he transformed from a mild-mannered salesman into a SUPER DESIGNER. I happened to have the outfit that I was wearing with me, and he asked to see it. He outfitted me from head to toe, including nail color selection to make everything POP! Little did I know that he was, in fact, a graphic designer with a gift for fashion design. When the day of the GALA came, I impressed myself. He became the one! When I think of shoes and fashion, I would stop at his counter first. Oh, yes… I have his number to ensure he will be there before I make the trip. He is the one!!!

Fashion. IT. Banking. Teaching. It goes for any and every industry sector.

You know what I'm going to ask… How can you tier your career to be strategically ready to expand your capacity? Gauge where you are and take *this* challenge. Become the one!"

There are only a few ways to receive a significant increase in your income that I am aware of which doesn't involve bank robbing… Don't try that at ALL! Either you are going to CREATE a lucrative business, of which there are several models, shift from one company to another and negotiate well a salary based on marketplace value of your skillset or shift inside the company where you already work demonstrating the value you bring. Either way, the word VALUE comes to my mind. Friends, there are companies that have employees who get paid minimum wage. What these employees bring to the table can be seen as disposable. What they do can be taught in a matter of days if not hours to someone else. From the human standpoint, they are VALUABLE but, organizationally, someone else can do their job TODAY. Then at that same company and on that same PAYROLL, there is that person who is paid handsomely; tens of thousands even on a monthly basis. Their time is of VALUE to the company and could not be replaced on a whim. That person is also valued on a human level. Yet, organizationally, their VALUE is HUGE.

Many of us fall somewhere in the middle of these two examples. I want to always lean toward the upper end of that spectrum. How about you?

✓ Check up

The temperature of the current marketplace is that many professionals, regardless of how good they are and how much value they bring to their employer, they can still find themselves being marginalized or even laid off due to business decisions. On a scale of 1 to 10, where do you believe your value at your current place of employment rests? One being, um…., this question concerns me because I see myself in my role as a part of the "pack" or ten being, the company would really think twice or even three times before questioning the overall usefulness and impact of my contributions to the company. ____

℞ Prescription

There are several DOSES to take into consideration right here: ATTITUDE, INTELLIGENCES, EDUCATION, ZEST, RELEVANCE, COMMUNICATION, PRESENTATION, and NETWORKING.

Okay. I'm going to suggest going through each of the prescriptions for these. Because you have to do it! <smile>

Add to these a possible conversation with your immediate supervisor/manager regarding the current "temperature" of your team. Ask, given your role, what one professional skill would they suggest you work on as you continue to be an integral part of the team. Seek to spend at least two hours a week learning/perfecting that skill.

Respect yourself enough to walk away from anything that no longer serves you, grows you, or makes you happy. If you aren't being treated with love and respect, check your price tag. Maybe you've marked yourself down. It's you who tells people what your worth is. Get off of the clearance rack and get behind the glass where they keep the valuables. – Anonymous

Dose 23

Worth

I know that we've talked about bringing VALUE to a company and beginning to show our VALUE. These are the externals that people see. This has to do with our skillset, EDUCATION and the like. Yet, this dose is about the YOU on the inside; how you feel about the person you are and your self-WORTH. This is also called your self-image.

Self-image and self-WORTH are huge keys to who we are in the marketplace and more of who we really are.

Our self-WORTH does determine how things play out in the "REAL" of our lives. This is the heart of who we are. There are a lot of people who are financially well off, but their self-WORTH or lack thereof is what propelled them to attain the money because their own perspective of who they are is tied up in how much money they have and what others may think of them. Is there anything wrong with money? ABSOLUTELY NOT! Does it mean that a person who has money is using it to hide who they are or who they feel they are not? ABSOLUTELY NOT. Self-worth is more than that.

It's in how we think and what we believe about who we are. Do we feel that we deserve happiness and wellbeing in life?

How can we ensure that our self-WORTH is where we should be? Start with putting life in perspective. You cannot compare yourself to anyone else. Even those with whom you may have grown up. Why? Because we are all UNIQUE and have different purpose on the planet. We cannot find our WORTH even in the families we were brought up in, even though that might give us some "meaning".

It still doesn't give us *our* WORTH. We have to know that as a person we are important. What we feel is important and that what we want is important. Look to yourself and the GOD force within you to know that. No externals can add to who YOU really are.

As you think about your career. Remember that you are not what the company says you are, nor are you what the paycheck reflects who you are to them. You are a person WORTHY of respect and appreciation. So many times I have heard a client or workshop attendee say, "I am ONLY a _____ (Fill in the blank)." This means that because their job does not seem as important as another's job, that they themselves are not as important. Not the case. I look at each person as important.

Ask yourself, would you speak to the CEO differently than a person in the maintenance sector? I hope that the answer is no. Why? Because they are both human beings and are WORTHY of respect. Sure, their jobs are different; different level of responsibility in the scheme of things, but it doesn't place more importance on who we are in this world. We are all important.

You might say, Janice, that is easy to say in this book. But in the real world, people put more importance and prestige on certain roles. Yes, I agree. It's the role.

Come on and show the world who you are! In her poem, Our

Deepest Fear, Marianne Williamson sums it up by saying, "there's nothing enlightening about playing small so that others will feel comfortable around us."

You are WORTHY because you are a representation of life that is to be lived. And for no other reason, let us GLORY in that. EVERYTHING ELSE we do, which is a by-product of who we are, is a bonus. If we pull together the strength of the 26 Doses here, we can surely be able to deliver some by-products that will be able to blow the minds of those we know and the world around us. But it does truly start right here. This should have been first, but, it could not be because… It starts with a "W".

✓ Check up

Generally when you receive a genuine compliment from someone do you typically feel okay with it, smile, thank them and move on or do you find a way to minimize their comment(s) by giving a reason/excuse for what they mentioned like saying, "Oh. This old thing," or feel slightly out of sorts for a bit of time to recover in your own head? The first scenario or the second?

℞ Prescription

If you shy away and do not feel worthy of attention, accolades, good things, wealth, love, promotions, you are not alone. Free yourself. This will hinder you from moving forward in your career and in life at some point. Here's step one, get a copy of OUR DEEPEST FEAR, by Marianne Williamson. It is a great poem that will be a bedrock for you as you move from here.

Secondly make a practice of saying good things about yourself.

If you catch yourself minimizing your achievements and/or abilities, stop yourself in your tracks, back up and say to yourself, "Hey, I am a really good _____." Ask a trusted colleague or friend to hold you accountable. This may also be a great time to create that BRAG book that I mentioned in LOSS/LOST DOSE.

The marketplace can assign VALUE but not that you are "VALUABLE". It cannot determine your WORTH. You are a person of excellence and purpose. You have to know that and always rest in that knowing.

26 Doses of Career Triage

You gotta know when to hold 'em. Know when to fold 'em. Know when to walk away. Know when to run. – Lyrics from the song in movie The Gambler

Dose 24

eXit

In the marketplace, there is always an ebb and flow. We as professionals need to learn to know where the tide is and when it is time for us to move on. Yes, having an EXIT strategy is important. We all would love to be in a work environment where we can find fulfillment and stay as long as our hearts desire. Kenny Roger said it best in the song, the Gambler:

"You gotta know when to hold 'em. Know when to fold 'em. Know when to walk away. Know when to run."

Yep!

Consider that when corporations are developing plans and things that they did not expect to occur like a major downturn in the market, they may have to make some hard decisions. One of those decisions might be to lay off some individuals or even an entire division. If this has ever happened to you, as it has to me, know that it is not necessarily a nice feeling. But it is real! They have told you that without your permission, it is time to move on.

Consider, my friend, that you are the CEO of YOU, Inc. You are now charged with ensuring that your career serves you well. You are at the forefront of making decisions with a high level of EMOTIONAL INTELLIGENCE. Decide the course of action to take about your EDUCATION, your WORTH, your MENTOR(S), your NETWORK and so on. I guarantee you that as you move along this path, there will be OPPORTUNITIES that will come your way like a fork in the road.

I could not help myself! ☺

Go right or go left. Stop! Wait... Move with caution.

If you are doing the right things you will have your eyes on what the market is doing and the EXIT you're considering is just what you want and are getting ready to do. You might have to put on your BRAVERY hat because it may be time to go. This can be scary sometimes but it is a satisfying thing to know that you have a decision to make. It's your call. It does not always have to be that the corporate layoff made the decision for you, which means it was NOT an option.

It's time to move on.

If you have done the right NETWORKING things along the way, you will be able to stay in connection with your old colleagues as you move on to that next chapter of your career.

But it is EXIT. Stage left. Or stage right.

Here is the thing I know some felt as soon as I said it. "I don't want to leave my team high and dry." Don't think of it that way. Consider it this way. If you don't move on, firstly, you will not know/experience the OPPORTUNITY on the other side of this move. Secondly, there is someone in the wings waiting for the position left vacant by you. If you don't leave, both of you will be out of your places.

Your responsibility is to leave your position/responsibilities in order and maintain the relationships that matter. People will jokingly say that they are upset with you for moving on but those who have your best interest at heart will really be glad that you are GROWING and GOING. Some wise person said, "The people who matter won't mind and the people who mind don't really matter."

It may feel strange to make this type of decision, but you do want and need it to be on your own terms. Hopefully, not because people are getting on your nerves but because it is a move that is a part of the plan.

Additionally, you may also look at any activities and other professional involvements that may have run their course. There are seasons for everything. You may be involved in a professional club or association that you feel is no longer suitable for where you are in your career, this also could be a reason for an EXIT. Take this as permission to look at how to successfully change the status of your participation with them to make way for new interests to blossom and direct you into your purpose.

✓ Check up

Generally when you receive a genuine compliment from someone do you typically feel okay with it, smile, thank them and move on or do you find a way to minimize their comment(s) by giving a reason/excuse for what they mentioned like saying, "Oh. This old thing," or feel slightly out of sorts for a bit of time to recover in your own head? The first scenario or the second? _____said in last chapter_____

℞ Prescription

Determine your professional priorities at this time: salary, upward mobility, reasonable security ☺, benefits, work hours/flexibility and so forth. Is your current place of employment satisfying you based on your priorities? Before making a move, do your due diligence to find out if you can stay where you are and make the professional head way you'd like to make. If the answer is no, are you ready to begin the possibly long journey of a job search? If yes, hold onto your hat. You should then take into consideration the DOSES of NETWORKING, PRESENTATION, DETERMINATION, VALUE, ATTITUDE, WORTH, INTELLIGENCES, BRAVERY, COMMUNICATION, EDUCATION and... Well I think you may have to go hard in the paint. Get ready. EXIT stage left but NOT without a new job in hand.

Additionally, if you are leveling up your game there may need to be a reconsideration of your current affiliations. List them in your notebook and determine if they are still viable for you or do you need to gracefully move on to other organizations or roles within your current organization that would help you to grow.

It's never too late to become what you might have been –
George Eliot

Dose 25

Youthfulness/Years

This is an age-old issue for society. Pun intended.

The age thing. Let's face it. We are all adding days to our lives. This is indeed a great thing. Getting older is a fact of life. However, it does not mean that we have to fall into the idea that our age impacts the fact we can still be viable in this workplace if that's where we find ourselves right now.

When I was 57, I told my daughter, Stephanie that 57 is the new 27. I just do it with 30 years' experience. And I mean that. I feel that I can lean into my age with grace and not carry it as an albatross. I use it to my advantage when that is warranted.

There are a lot of clichés around, the biggest of which is that age is only a number. That is true. But then why is that we try so desperately to hide our age? With the dates on our resumes? Or no dates on our resumes?

Being older. Being younger. Each has its benefits. AND the things that can work against us. If you take to heart the other doses that I have shared so far and the one to come, you will see that the impact of your YOUTH may not be as much of a negative thing.

I once participated in a series of workshops with a colleague. Part of the training was around age diversity in the workplace. It was a phenomenal segment eye-opening program. The group was indeed very diverse as a lot of workplaces are today. The largest group was the Baby Boomers. Then the Gen-X'ers, the Millennials and the mid-sixties (aka Veterans).

We did an exercise that was based around perceptions. Each group listed positives and the negatives about the other groups. This was quite a lovely activity with a lot of great discussions.

What did we as the facilitator, and me as a career professional learn in this process? You guessed it. EVERY age group has its pluses and minuses. If we can be EMOTIONALLY INTELLIGENT about it, then we can learn to leverage everyone's strengths to benefit the employer and the employees as well.

In the midst of a job search? Am I too old? Am I too young? This may seem to be the case. I have found ways to navigate these seemingly real things. One of the best ways is through NETWORKING. Your NETWORK can get you in front of the right people in the right companies by bypassing what might be prejudgments of those looking at resumes coming across their desks. The reality is that there are prejudgments that can keep the RIGHT candidate from getting an interview. The personal touch of a NETWORKED introduction can help in this instance.

We must learn how to use our YEARS to our advantage. If you are a professional with 30 years' experience as an administrative professional, consider how much you have seen and how many FIRES you put out in your day. You can be able to show the strength of your experience to those around you. Don't rest on your longevity thinking that just because you know people that they know/understand what you actually bring to the table. They don't, unless you show them. You've got to be your own cheerleader. Not in an arrogant way but with confidence. Arrogance is pushy and aggressive but confidence is assertive and kind. You CAN show your VALUE. You can rest in your own WORTH as you move along in your organization.

As a young professional, you may be fighting what seems to be an uphill battle because people may not take you seriously or you may not have the proof of your abilities to help you demonstrate the VALUE you can bring to a work environment. How can you step past that? I have several suggestions that can move you beyond your peers. You can leverage the influence of a MENTOR. Also, reach into your NETWORK to find those who can help you identify work that is suitable for your skillset but that has the POTENTIAL for greater OPPORTUNITIES.

As a professional who has little experience, it will be important for you to pull out every experience you have had, skills and abilities that will be attractive to an employer. You may also be able to do this if you have VOLUNTEER experience. Yes, this can count. In the world of work, it is not necessarily where you have obtained the skill but proving that you can use that skill well.

In our quest to be able to be viable in the marketplace, we must be able to PRESENT ourselves well. If you are younger, then be that! Happily! Project your abilities/strengths and that you are ready to put in the time and energy to help the company's growth. If you are more mature, be that! Convey that the capabilities and strengths you have are RELEVANT and VALUABLE to an organization's need for continued stability and growth in the marketplace.

You may notice that my focus in the last paragraph is on how you will benefit the organization. That's right. The truth of the matter is, they don't want to know that you are "willing to learn" more than what are you able to do for them. Although there is an opportunity for learning in a work environment, they will always hang their hats on what you CAN DO primarily. Not what you will do because that can come later. Position yourself to the tune of what you bring to the game. Yes, the growth will come.

Regardless of the generation you are in, you have a great reservoir of skills that you offer and for the right employer. Do your due diligence to be RIGHT for the RIGHT on. Put to use all of the doses and you will see the results you are looking for.

✓   Check up

Do you feel that your age is a less than positive factor in how people treat you on your job or in your ability to get the employment that you desire? Yes or No? _____

R̲X̲ Prescription

Regardless of which end of the spectrum you find yourself, now is the time to set things straight. Whether you are just entering into the work force or you are a seasoned professional, you can find the work environment and job where you can add VALUE and obtain satisfaction.

Let's start with your being able to articulate your UNIQUE SELLING POINT (USP). What do you do extremely well? Toot your own horn in a positive uplifting way. For example as a Business Analyst I bring the business needs of a company together with the capabilities of technology to help a company succeed in the marketplace.

_____

_____

I intend to live forever Or die trying. — Groucho Marx

Dose 26

Zeal

ZEAL is not a word that is commonly used in today's world. It seems to be equated with some that are overboard. That would be absolutely correct. We are talking about radical change in this book. ZEAL is a very appropriate word and I want us to see our lives from the standpoint of being over the top - OTT!

Being ZEALOUS with regard to our career is going to land us in great places. It goes hand in hand with DETERMINATION and FOCUS. Zeal is that fire that you are going to need to bring to everything that you do.

Webster's definition of ZEAL is great energy or enthusiasm in pursuit of a cause or an objective.

If you don't have it, now is the right time to develop it. I believe that you can. Will others think that you have lost it? Well, you don't need to know what others are going to think about you. This is *your* career.

I have always said that I absolutely LOVE what I do. I mean that. I have had the opportunity to work alongside great professionals. I have the opportunity to meet and support amazing professionals. Some of them are yet to agree that they are amazing but nonetheless, they are amazing. I have the opportunity to use the gifts and talents that I have been blessed with to help people to become their best selves and I enjoy it. You really can't get any better than that. Yippee! What is there not to like.

And because this is in place, I have a ZEAL for what I do and I go after it with everything I've got. Hard in the paint as they would say in basketball.

Why is having ZEAL important for you in your career pursuits? It is because it is the fuel behind it all. It is the driving momentum that will push you through the tough times. When an OBSTACLE comes and you can see it ahead of you, your ZEAL, energy, will help you to take it on.

Have you ever been riding a bike and you look ahead and see that you are approaching an incline? What do you do about it? Well, there are a few things that come to mind. You can huff and puff your way up the hill with the same speed that you had as you were approaching it; you could get off of the bike and walk it up the incline at a restful state; or you could press into the incline by increasing your speed before you hit it and let the momentum of your speed move you along at a much more comfortable pace. The latter, pushing into it may actually take more energy at the outset. But the momentum of your efforts can actually make the incline a little easier to manage in the long run.

That's ZEAL.

As humans, we naturally ebb and flow in our feelings. That's an entire chapter I DID NOT include in this book. Feelings can slow us down. They can impact our perception of the things going on around us simply because of what is going on within us. When feelings come along, they can bring us DOWN. Normal. We must override that at some point. I will let you have a moment....

There. That's it. <smiles>

After the moment, you must dig deep inside for the ZEAL you have to carry you onto the next accomplishment, task, meeting or event. Your ZEAL is your DRIVING force and mind over matter.

When we embrace the fact that we have got this and we decide that we are going to be okay, allow THAT to inform our situation. Whatever is coming to us, we indeed can handle with the momentum of ZEAL.

I have used some other words here that are synonyms for ZEAL:

Passion | zealousness | committedness | ardor | love | fervor
fire | avidity | devotedness | enthusiasm | eagerness
keenness | appetite | taste | relish | gusto | devotion
vigor | energy | verve zest | fervency | ardency | fondness

I want you to feel this in your heart today. Why? Because, if you are in a space where your employment is not making you happy, you have to be able to strap on ZEAL like a superhero garment. Change from Clark Kent into SUPERMAN. OR Tony Starks into IRONMAN. Or Diana Prince into WONDER WOMAN. Harness yourself with the energy to make this career a work of art. ZEAL your way in and keep it going through the flames of your know-how and your WILL to get it done by putting blinders on to what your coworkers might say or think.

The first time I read Zig Ziglar's Top Performance, I went into a crazy mode. I decided that I was going to be an outstanding employee and do my absolute best. I planned how I was going to change how I recorded my workload. Why? In our workplace, as technical professionals, it was typical to pad the projects with extra time for the "what could be's of life". Not that there weren't things that could not happen unexpectedly, but I was being radically different. Remember? I went the radical route. I scaled down my time estimates by days and sometimes weeks depending on what it was. I was sure that these numbers were more accurate than they would have been using the previous method we used. It was routine that the senior programmers would review the plans to approve them before they went to the business clients. One day a senior employee reviewed my plan and came back to ask me what I was trying to do. She said that these numbers were doable BUT if I submit this, then it would put into question everyone else's numbers because mine were so tight. Basically, she was telling me to back off of the TOP PERFORMANCE way of thinking. Come to the "normal" side. I needed to stay average. Um…. This put me in a predicament. She and I had a conversation and we worked out an understanding of what I was trying to accomplish as a professional and how I no longer wanted to work status quo. She didn't like it and she let me know that in no uncertain terms, but she had to relinquish and approve my new numbers. Interestingly enough, no one else questioned my new approach but the client liked the fact that I did my projects more quickly than the others and would sometimes ask for me specifically when certain types of tasks would come along so I could handle them.

I decided to embrace ZEAL for the things that I did and it worked to my advantage.

I assure you that if you take on a new ZEAL for your life and your career, you will feel the wind in your face that will ultimately be at your back pushing you to new heights of professional and personal satisfaction in the days ahead.

✓ Check up

Do you feel that your age is a less than positive factor in how people treat you on your job or in your ability to get the employment that you desire? Yes or No? _____

 Prescription

Listen to a DOSE of each of these three gentlemen: Zig Ziglar, Jim Rohn or Earl Nightingale. They are old school and POWERFUL. Determine which of them you like best then follow through several of their programs or teaching on YouTube.

Determine that every day you will put ALL of you into the day. If you are not feeling 100% on a particular day, determine not to voice a complaint. Review the following DOSES of GRATITUDE, ATTITUDE, VALUE, JOY and WORTH.

The journey of a thousand miles begins with a single step.
– Lao Tzu

Conclusion

Welcome to the end! You made it with me! YES!

I trust that you have enjoyed these Doses. As you read about me and others in these pages, were you able to identify some aspects to focus on? And some aspects where you are doing well? I am confident of both. There are dangerous words that we should all avoid saying. They are, 'I know that." I believe that each of us should be ever learning especially because things change at the speed of thought. You know that's fast.

As it is with every journey of learning… There is a finale. This is like graduation. I can hear the traditional echoes of Sir Edward Elgar's *Pomp and Circumstance* being beautifully played right now. The exciting part about a commencement is that the word itself means beginning. So each of you are now at a new and exciting place in your career.

In the Preface of the *26 Doses of Career Triage*, I outlined some significant things regarding next steps. The treatment plans are simple but POWERFUL. Do not be fooled. The efficacy of these 26 Doses does rest on your EFFORT. I have heard it said if you get a gym membership but don't go to the gym you cannot call it a scam. **We must do the work**. Look at the plans and determine what fits your situation. Work through them and BUILD your career so that it can be resilient in this ever-changing marketplace.

Needless to say, do your due diligence to be ready with the tools you need to bring to the marketplace such as your resume and your Dynamic Networking Intro. If and when I see you, I will be sure to say, "Tell me about yourself." Do not let me down! <smiles>

You are moving into the treatment and recovery phase of this

TRIAGE journey. Do your due diligence. Treat yourself well. Follow up and follow through.

Stay in touch and PLEASE share your journey with me from time to time.

Here's to a healthy career!

Janice

Dynamic Networking Intro

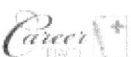

Make this yours...

My name is _____
(Do not add Titles and credentials here)

'I _____'
(What do the people who receive your product/service receive after you have done a good job?
The pie in the sky description)

Most recently/currently I worked at/I work at _____

As a _____
(This is your specific role)

Use this as the Follow up in your conversation or Interview add in:

I help people/organizations to _____
(What's are two specific things that the people who receive your product/service are able to do now?)

I am most passionate/excited about using my _____

_____ skills

I am at my best when I _____
(If you could wave a 'magic wand' this would be the only thing you'd do)

I am currently seeking to _____
(What's your two primary professional goals for a new and an additional job?)

_____

_____

Leave them informed but asking for and wanting more....

Perfect Practice Makes Perfect ~ Janice Coleman, President/CEO
Janice Coleman Corporation

janice@janicecoleman.com   609-594-2244

26 Doses of Career Triage

Quotealogue

Attitude

Our attitude toward life determines life's attitude toward us – John N. Mitchell

Bravery

Cowards die a thousand deaths. But the brave only die once. – Ernest Hemingway

Communications

Communication is a skill that you can learn. It's like riding a bicycle or typing. If you're willing to work at it, you can rapidly improve the quality of every part of your life. – Brian Tracy

Determination

If you can't fly then run, if you can't run then walk, if you can't walk then crawl, but whatever you do you keep moving forward. – Rev. Dr. Martin Luther King

Education

Live as if you were to die tomorrow. Learn as if you were to live forever. — Mahatma Gandhi

Focus

Whenever you want to achieve something, keep your eyes open, concentrate and make sure you know exactly what it is you want. No one can hit their target with their eyes closed. — Paulo Coelho, <u>The Devil and Miss Prym</u>

Gratitude
Give thanks with a grateful heart. Give thanks because of what the Lord has done for us. – Give Thanks by Don Moen and Paul Wilbur

Health
The greatest health is wealth - Virgil

Intelligences
If your emotional abilities aren't in hand, if you don't have self-awareness, if you are not able to manage your distressing emotions, if you can't have empathy and have effective relationships, then no matter how smart you are, you are not going to get very far. – Daniel Goleman

Joy
If you can't find joy in the path you are on and what you are working toward now, how do you expect to find joy once you get there? – Anonymous

Kinetic
You were born to win, but to be a winner, you must plan to win, prepare to win, and expect to win. – Zig Ziglar

Loss / Lost
If you want to <u>grow and develop yourself</u>, embrace failure. If you want to become the best at what you do, you've got to be willing to fail, again and again. And then finally, one day, you can fail your way to greatness. – Les Brown

Mentoring
Show me a successful individual and I'll show you someone who had real positive influences in his or her life. I don't care what you do for a living— if you do it well I'm sure there was someone cheering you on or showing the way. A mentor. – Denzel Washington

Networking

If you want to go fast, go alone. If you want to go far, go with others. — African Proverb

Obstacles/Opportunity

When we are no longer able to change a situation - we are challenged to change ourselves. — Viktor Frankl

Presentation

If you're presenting yourself with confidence, you can pull off pretty much anything. — Katy Perry

Quality/Quantity

Quality means doing it right when no one is looking. — Henry Ford

Relevance

Change before you have to. — Jack Welch

Success

Success is doing what you have been designed to do and doing it well. — Janice Coleman

Time

God's Minute: I've only just a minute,
Only sixty seconds in it.
Forced upon me, can't refuse it,
Didn't seek it, didn't choose it,
But it's up to me to use it.
I must suffer if I lose it,
Give an account if I abuse it,
Just a tiny little minute,
But eternity is in it. — Dr. Benjamin E. Mays

Uniqueness
Be YOU! There is no competition. – Unknown

Value
My goal has always been to add value, not to be redundant, not to get in the way, but to do things that lift and move things forward in a very strategic and objective way so that there are real outcomes. – Michelle Obama

Worth
Respect yourself enough to walk away from anything that no longer serves you, grows you, or makes you happy. If you aren't being treated with love and respect, check your price tag. Maybe you've marked yourself down. It's you who tells people what your worth is. Get off of the clearance rack and get behind the glass where they keep the valuables. – Anonymous

eXit
You gotta know when to hold 'em. Know when to fold 'em. Know when to walk away. Know when to run. – Kenny Rogers from the song the Gambler

Youthfulness/Years
It's never too late to become what you might have been. – George Eliot

Zeal
I intend to live forever Or die trying – Groucho Marx

ABOUT THE AUTHOR

Janice Coleman is a lover of people who is 'Preparing People to Perform', by providing customized training/keynote speeches, career coaching and innovative events. With over a decade of experience in Information Technology, Janice has led teams of IT professionals in the Greater Philadelphia Region over those years. Janice transitioned into the Education and Training Industry where she has been able to leverage her technical experience with her marketplace knowledge/savvy. This includes the disciplines of leadership, communications and teambuilding. She has helped executive leaders and their teams be more viable partners to their business counterparts in the context of their unique industries.

Janice has helped many professionals to increase their value and improve their career outlook in a powerful way. These have yielded many successes with measurable results across a wide variety of corporations and nonprofit organizations. Janice Coleman presents a power packed message and an informative presentation to enhance and ignite professionals to a new level of value-added capacity. Over the years she has influenced and inspired thousands to embrace the best version of themselves.

Janice has a degree in Christian Ministry as well as several professional certificates in career coaching, computer technology, project management, communications and leadership.

She resides in New Jersey with her family, hailing from the great city of Philadelphia PA. She is an avid reader, soon to be world traveler, longtime lover of music and a reemerging jazz saxophonist.

CONTACT JANICE

To book Janice as a speaker for your next event
or
For a 30-minute Career Triage consultation
Contact Janice at
janice@janicecoleman.com | 609.594.2244

www.ingramcontent.com/pod-product-compliance
Lightning Source LLC
Chambersburg PA
CBHW060843170526
45158CB00001B/223